DIMENSIONS OF THE HOLOCAUST

Lectures at Northwestern University

Elie Wiesel
Lucy S. Dawidowicz
Dorothy Rabinowitz
Robert McAfee Brown

NORTHWESTERN UNIVERSITY
Evanston, Illinois

Printed in the United States of America

FOREWORD

The study of history has many functions—to preserve and transmit the shape of the past, to rectify the record in the face of falsehood and prejudice, and above all to probe and ponder the meaning of human events. It is now over thirty years since the government of Nazi Germany systematically and with clinical ruthlessness set about exterminating European Jewry, and an entire generation has grown up for whom the Holocaust is little more than the tearful babbling of voices entombed in the documents of the past. It is clearly time that the story was retold, for it is the prime obligation of the historian to combat indifference and to preserve the message of history so that men and women cannot be said to have lived, suffered and died in vain. It is also the task of the scholar to set the record straight. There are always those who, for reasons of their own, seek to deny or distort or subvert the evidence, and from the start the Holocaust has had its apologists, its distorters, and its deniers. There is only one way of answering the prejudice, misrepresentation and confusion perpetrated by those who traffic in untruth, and that is to set good scholarship against bad so that everyone can judge the evidence for himself.

Finally, the essence of good history is not simply to label, document, footnote and describe what happened but also to point out that every historical event has dimensions far beyond its simple existence in time. There is the documented record but there is also the living memory, the moral implication, and the imaginative impact that the past has upon the present. The truth of the Holocaust is not limited to counting the number of murders committed as a result of a calculated act of state policy; it is also the realization that such an atrocity to humanity is an issue of conscience. As Elie Wiesel has said: "The Holocaust was so immense, so incredible that it is a unique event. There can be no other event like it."

1

Uniqueness and magnitude raise profound moral and metaphysical problems. To assign causes, to set an event in history and to perceive it in terms of historical perspective, appears to belittle it and to make it common. Moreover, to offer an explanation for the murder of six million Jews is to assert far more than the simple fact that the atrocity occurred. It suggests that it is possible for any society, given the right conditions, to create such a barbarity; that the Holocaust is a product of human history; and that it can somehow be made to fit into the ultimate design of an all-knowing deity. Furthermore, causation, be it human or divine, implies the possibility that things might have been otherwise, and inevitably the Holocaust arouses feelings of guilt in Christians and Jews alike for man's failure and God's apparent indifference. The only explanation of the genuinely unique is no explanation at all: it happened because it happened. Yet the core of all good scholarship, indeed the function of any university, is to seek, if not the simple explanation, at least a sense of understanding, a comprehension of the Holocaust in terms of all of its dimensions: of how it came about, of how it seared and shaped the lives of its survivors, of how it posed moral and philosophical questions about man's nature and God's purpose, and of how it must remain forever a reminder that it can never be allowed to happen again.

For all these reasons the administration made funds available so that its history department could sponsor a series of lectures which by chance fell during that week in April when the Warsaw Ghetto Uprising is traditionally commemorated. Four specialists spoke their minds on a subject which is one of the most significant, complex and tragic events of Western history. Each brought to the Holocaust a distinct dimension. The first speaker, Professor Elie Wiesel, spoke as the historian's ally, the creative genius who by literary artistry can bring the past with all of its pettiness, anguish and sacrifices to life by assigning motives and actions and giving meaning to dead events. He stands as evidence that Zelig Kalmanovich's words to the men and women of the Vilna Ghetto would not go unheeded: "Your struggles for humanity will inspire poems." As a witness to the Holocaust, Professor Wiesel is consumed by the historian's obsession that the vision of the past must be shared by all men lest it be forgotten. Professor Lucy Dawidowicz, the second lecturer, spoke on the Holocaust as historical record, the indispensable raw material upon which historical truth is grounded, showing how the historian goes about his appointed task: "the exact, impartial, critical investigation of events," and their integration into a dramatic and living totality. The third lecture was presented by Dorothy Rabinowitz who spoke on the Holocaust as living memory, the record of the lives of those who carry with them testimony from their own suffering. Reserved for the last was Professor Robert McAfee Brown who struggled with that most difficult dimension—the Holocaust as a problem in moral choice. It was his task to probe, if not to answer, the unanswerable: the place of the Holocaust in the ultimate meaning of man's world and God's design.

There is a dread that haunts us all, the fear that not only will the Holocaust be forgotten but, worse, that it will become a matter of indifference—a meaningless, senseless, inexplicable horror. It is Northwestern University's hope that these four lectures—four dimensions of the Holocaust —will open the door to greater understanding and will stand as a permanent witness to an event which must never be allowed to be forgotten so that it will never occur again.

Lacey Baldwin Smith
Chairman of the History Department

August 1977

Elie Wiesel

Through his books and lectures, Elie Wiesel has become an eloquent spokesman for Jews in the United States and throughout the world. His books speak for themselves. They include: *The Oath; Souls on Fire; One Generation After; A Begger in Jerusalem; Legends of Our Time; The Jews of Silence; The Gates of the Forest; The Town Beyond the Wall; The Accident; Night;* and *Dawn.*

Born in Transylvania, Mr. Wiesel was still a child when taken to Birkenau, Auschwitz, Monowitz and Buchenwald. Liberated by the American Army, he went to Paris, where he studied at the Sorbonne. After working as a journalist and writer, he came to the United States in 1956.

University Professor and Andrew W. Mellon Professor in the Humanities at Boston University, Mr. Wiesel has won numerous literary awards in France and the United States.

He has received honorary degrees from the Jewish Theological Seminary, Yeshiva University, Hebrew Union College, Marquette University, Hofstra University, Boston University, Manhattanville College, Simmons College, Spertus College of Judaica and Bar-Ilan University in Israel.

THE HOLOCAUST
AS LITERARY INSPIRATION
by Elie Wiesel

First, a few words about tonight. I shall speak to you as a Jew, a witness and a writer, and the three are fused into one. I belong to a people whose suffering is the most ancient in the world. I belong to a people whose memory keeps that suffering alive. I belong to a people who tried to curtail that suffering. Limit it. Disarm it and, in a way, humanize it. Mr. Chairman, you speak of history, we are a people of history. I think we have invented historicity if not history. I belong to a people that remembers. No other people remembers as well both our friends and our enemies as we do. *"Zachor v'shamor b'dibur echad . . ."* We are told, "Remember and observe" were given in one word. Just as all the days were created for one day alone, the Sabbath, all the other words were created and given for one word alone, "Remember."

Now, a few words about myself. Some 33 years ago (April 1944) a very young boy, extremely religious, extremely naive and innocent, arrived into a kingdom that was a kingdom of curse and malediction. A kingdom of night. He saw people and he saw flames and he did not know that the two would meet before his very eyes. They walked, he and his father, and they walked and they walked into that night toward the flames. Then a man came to them and said, "You know, soon you shall be there, soon you shall die in the flames." And that little boy turned to his father and said, "It is impossible. I don't believe it. It cannot be. After all we are in the middle of the twentieth century, the world would not remain silent." That boy was wrong. The world *was* silent. That boy was convinced later that were he to survive, he would tell the tale; he was convinced that if he would tell the tale history would be redeemed. Man would undergo a total metamorphosis, something of the Messiah would appear in every man— simply because the tale would be told. Part of the tale was told and man did not change. What that boy could not have imagined then, and nobody has imagined since, was that one day the story would be denied altogether. That one day he would have to stand here before you and simply tell you, "Yes, it was true." Professor Smith, you used many words, you spoke of absurdities, of truth. There is one word you did not mention because I think you are a delicate spirit. And that word is "obscenity." What a man in this community of scholars did was nothing less than speak obscenely, nothing less than bring shame to this community.

Now a few words about the tale. Our tale was not about Jews alone. It was about what had been done to Jews by others. And because of its magnitude and its ontological nature, the Holocaust therefore will forever remain a challenge to this generation and perhaps to all generations. Some of us have chosen to stay within its fiery walls so as to explore and perhaps redeem its hidden truth. Whatever we do, whatever we say, must be measured against its background. If at times we sound oversensitive to certain words, if at times we overreact to certain events, it is that we have chosen to remember the time when Jews seem to have been forgotten by all men.

And now, a few words about the event itself. Its centrality in our lives and in history has not been disputed except by some insensitive and deranged minds who should arouse both pity and disgust. The Event, with a capital "E," weighs on our conscience and consciousness. Whatever we may do or undo, we are motivated by what took place in that faraway kingdom of darkness. Whatever we may hope to achieve or relinquish, to reveal or suppress, our eyes will forever see the invisible universe where God and man looked at one another with fear, not with pride. As seen against that background, all that can be obtained through knowledge has to be recalled into question. After Auschwitz words are no longer innocent. After Treblinka silence is filled with new meaning. After Majdanek madness has recaptured its mystical appeal. As a result man's relationship to his creator, to society, to politics, to literature, to his fellow man and to himself has to be reexamined. The event robbed man of all his masks. On the side of the executioner all the representatives of organized society were there. For the factories of death to emerge and function, philosophers and psychologists, scholars and engineers, attorneys and aristocrats, lovers of art and poetry, criminals and sadists had to join forces. It was a joint venture on their part. Similarly, all categories were included among the victims as well. No one was spared, no one pitied. All Jews were marked, singled out, doomed, massacred not for what they had done or acquired but simply for what they were, Jews. Their being was the target to be destroyed. All Jews everywhere shared the same fate, old and young, rich and poor, beggars and princes, children and their grandparents, all had to disappear. Those who took up arms and fought and also those who did not. Those who had the strength to resist and also those who chose to die in prayer. Over there even the heroes perished as victims and even the victims were heroes. And there were so many that they could people an entire kingdom, which indeed they did. Theirs was the kingdom of night. Forgotten by God, forsaken by Him, they lived alone, suffered alone, fought alone. Alone they faced mighty legions, the mightiest in Europe then. Alone. That is the key word, the haunting theme. Alone with no allies, no friends, totally, desperately alone. During the uprising of the Warsaw Ghetto, its commander-in-chief, Mordechai Anielewicz, a young man in his early twenties, wrote to his friend Antek Zukerman on the outside, "As we feel our last days approaching, we ask you to remember how we have been betrayed." Yes, they were betrayed. The world knew and kept silent and their solitude then was matched only by God's. Mankind let them down. Mankind let them suffer and agonize and perish alone. And yet, and yet, they did not die alone, for something in all of us died with them.

And now a few words about the literature of the Holocaust or about literary inspiration. There is no such thing, not with Auschwitz in the equation. "The Holocaust as Literary Inspiration" is a contradiction in terms. As in everything else, Auschwitz negates all systems, destroys all doctrines. They cannot but impoverish the experience which lies beyond our reach. Ask any survivor and he will tell you, and his children will tell you. He or she who did not live through the event will never know it. And he or she who did live through the event will never reveal it. Not entirely. Not really. Between our memory and its reflection there stands a wall that cannot be pierced. The past belongs to the dead and the survivor does not recognize himself in the words linking him to them. We speak in code, we survivors, and this code cannot be broken, cannot be deciphered, not by you no matter how much you try. A novel about Treblinka is either not a novel or not about Treblinka. A novel about Majdanek is about blasphemy. *Is* blasphemy. Treblinka means death, absolute death, death of language and of hope, death of trust and of inspiration. Its secret is doomed to remain intact. How can one write about a situation which goes beyond its very description? How can one write a novel about the Holocaust? How can one write about a situation and not identify with all its characters? And how can one identify with so many victims? Worse, how can one identify with the executioner? How could a victim say "I" in the place of his killer? Furthermore, how can one convince himself without feeling guilty that he may use such events for literary purposes? Wouldn't that mean, then, that Treblinka and Belzec, Ponar and Babi Yar all ended in fantasy, in words, in beauty, that it was simply a matter of literature?

A matter of words. What kind of words? That, too, became a difficulty the writer had to solve and overcome. Language had been corrupted to the point that it had to be invented anew and purified. This time we wrote not with words but against words. Often we told less so as to make the truth more credible. Had any one of us told the whole story, he would have been proclaimed mad. Once upon a time the novelist and the poet were in advance of their readers. Not now. Once upon a time the artist could foresee the future. Not now. Now he has to remember the past, knowing all the while that what he has to say will never be told. What he hopes to transmit can never be transmitted. All he can possibly hope to achieve is to communicate the impossibility of communication. No wonder, then, that after the war there were poets and novelists who chose to commit suicide. Paul Celan in Paris, Beno Wertzberger in Israel, Tadeusz Borowski in Poland, Yosef Wulff in Berlin. Some succumbed temporarily to insanity as did Nelly Sachs, or turned to science fiction, or stopped writing novels.

Just as readers would commit suicide in the nineteenth century, writers did in ours, because they felt impotent. They realized that once you have penetrated the kingdom of night you have reached the end. There is nothing else to discover. There is nothing else to say. There is nothing else to do. You remain a prisoner forever. So they felt inadequate and guilty. They thought they had said something. No, they had said nothing. It was simply too much for the survivor. Too much to try and fulfill his mission. He had to invent a new life for his characters, to compose a new rhythm, a new song, a new *niggun,* and maybe a new memory, a new texture to express the ineffable and uncover parts of the secret so jealously guarded by so many dead. Most novelists of this category, or most writers, seem to have followed the same pattern. Viewing literature as a way to correct injustices, they wrote their tales so as to protest against what was done to their friends, to their families, to their own childhood and to their people.

Theirs was meant to be a powerful protest against society and its rules, its cruelty and its indifference. Their aim was not only to describe the massacre but also to paint what preceded it. The life, the peacefulness of the family, the joy of its holidays, the charm of its fools and the wisdom of its children. They wrote their memoirs so as to bring back to life people and places destroyed by the executioner and to prove that Jews can, with words, build upon ruins. That is why the *shtetl,* the little village of eastern Europe that became the illustration of our kingdom, holds such fascination for them. What is the *shtetl* if not Jerusalem away from Jerusalem? And it has survived in words alone. And those innumerable cities and villages where ten generations of Jews had sanctified their exile through study and prayer, they are gone for good, erased from geography. The *shtetl*, that small kingdom of fire erected and purified in fire, has disappeared forever. Nowadays we have Jewish cities, capitals, settlements, suburbs and even military bases, but we do not have the *shtetl* and never will. It was swallowed up by smoke and night along with its sages and their pupils, its preachers and their followers, its dreamers and their dreams. Here the hangman's victory seems final. Wiped out for good. The *shtetl* can be found only in song, only in memory, only in words, in words alone. That is why the teller of its tale does whatever he can to present it in its most glorious aspect. Let the executioner know what he has destroyed. What is said of Judaism is true of the *shtetl*. It must be approached from its most exalting angle. The result: survivors wrote magnificently about their past, about the *shtetl*, about their pre-Holocaust period. But not about the Holocaust. It's simple. One cannot write about the Holocaust. Not if you are a writer.

Understandably, the theme evoked some sacred awe in literature. It was considered taboo, for the initiated alone. The great novelists of our time—Malraux, Mauriac, Faulkner, Silone, Mann and Camus—chose to stay away from it. It was their way of showing respect toward the dead and the survivors as well. Also it was their way of admitting their inability to cope with themes where imagination weighed less than experience. They were honest enough to realize that they are not to penetrate into a domain haunted by so many dead and buried under so many ashes. They chose not to describe something they could not fathom. But then there are the witnesses and there is their testimony. If the Greeks invented tragedy, the Romans the epistle, and the Renaissance the sonnet, our generation invented a new literature, that of testimony. We have all been witnesses and we all feel we have to bear testimony for the future. And that became an obsession, the single most powerful obsession that permeated all the lives, all the dreams, all the work of those people. One minute before they died they thought that was what they had to do.

Chaim Kaplan wrote in his diary on January 16, 1942, "The whole nation is sinking in a sea of horror and cruelty. I do not know whether anyone else is recording these daily events. The conditions of life which surround us are not conducive to such literary labors. Anyone who keeps such a record endangers his life. But it doesn't alarm me. I sense within me the magnitude of this hour and my responsibility to it. I have an inner awareness that I am fulfilling a national obligation. My words are not re-written. Momentary reflexes shape them. Perhaps their value lies in this. My record will serve as source material for the future historian."

He was wrong. Everybody wrote. Emmanuel Ringelblum gathered a committee of a hundred historians and that is what they did. They wrote. In every ghetto, as we shall see, and in every camp, as we shall see, there were historians. July 22, 1942, again Chaim Kaplan in Warsaw: "I haven't the strength to hold the pen in my hand. I am broken, shattered. My thoughts are jumbled. I don't know where to start or stop. I have seen Jewish Warsaw through over forty years of events but never before has she worn such a face. A whole community of 400,000 people condemned to exile. The street beggars were among the first to be deported. They were captured by the hundreds and taken away on transports—where to? No one knows, but everyone understands—to death. Their cries and wails ascended to the heart of the heavens. But who hears cries in the time of such destruction? I will stop now and go to bed, but it will be a sleepless night for I am one of those affected by the expulsion decree. It is possible that I shall not be privileged to end this chronicle on a note of consolation." July 31, 1942, Kaplan again: "My powers are insufficient to record all that is worthy of being recorded. Most of all I am worried that I may be consuming my strength for naught. Should I too be taken, all my effort will be wasted. My utmost concern is for hiding my diary so that it will be preserved for future generations. As long as my pulse beats I shall continue my sacred task." August 4, 1942, evening, Kaplan: "I have not yet been caught. I have not yet been evicted from my apartment. My building has not yet been confiscated. But only a step separates me from all these misfortunes. All day my wife and I take turns standing watch looking through the kitchen window which overlooks the courtyard to see if the blockade has begun. People run from place to place like madmen. Thousands of people in the Nalevke-Zammenhof block were driven from their homes and taken to the transfer point. More than thirty people were slaughtered. In the afternoon the fury subsided a bit; 13,000 people had been seized and sent off, among them 5,000 who went of their own free will. They had had their fill of the ghetto life, which is a life of hunger and fear of death. They escaped from the trap. I wish I could allow myself to do what they did. If my life ends, what will become of my diary?" The next day his life ended and miraculously his diary was preserved, and we are reading from it.

There were historians in every ghetto, chroniclers in every camp. Ringelblum and Kaplan, Marshal Rolnik and Anne Frank, Rabbi Shimon Huberband and Leo Weles, Yankel Wirnik and Alexander Donath. Every event had to be recorded and was. Ringelblum's committee had access to all sources in the Warsaw Ghetto. Rabbi Huberband roamed around ruins of smaller communities and brought back episodes of torment and persecution, and *kiddush ha-shem,* the sanctification of God's name. Leo Weles kept his diary inside Janowska. Wirnik wrote his shortly after his escape from Treblinka. The urge to bear witness was overwhelming. "Everybody is writing, writing," Ringelblum noted in his diary. Rabbis and scholars, merchants and cobblers, anonymous people—all served as historians, as witnesses to history.

The celebrated historian, Professor Simon Dubnow, as he was led to the execution place in Riga with his community, turned to his companions and urged them, "Open your eyes and your ears. Remember every word, every gesture, every outcry, every tear." He was killed but his words remained. Somebody remembered these words. Eugene Heimler, a psychiatrist, a young Hungarian Jewish boy, wrote in his memoir, "There were messages I had to deliver to the living from the dead. There were things I had to do. Words I had to speak. Moments which I had to dissect in order to show the world what I had seen and lived through. On behalf of the millions who had seen it also but could no longer speak of their dead, burned bodies, I would be the voice." There were chroniclers even among the *Sonderkommando,* the saddest of the sad victims who were forced to burn their brothers and sisters before sharing the same fate themselves. In diaries written with incredible power and beauty we read the testimony, which at times is of unbearable intensity. If ever I come close to total despair it is when I plunge into their tale. They describe the last moments of the victims already crowded in the gas chamber. They repeat their last words. They carry their last fears, and you want to cry. You want to weep. And then you read the words of a certain Zalman Gradowski: "Will I ever be able to cry again?" Listen well. Not laugh again. But cry again. And you contain your pain and you do not cry. It's hard, almost impossible to read, let alone read aloud. These pages of these diaries were found in the ashes. Then you say to yourself that if they had the courage and the desperate faith, if they had the strength to write such words, we must have the strength to read them. Zalman Gradowski's diaries contain several introductions, appeals to the person who will find the papers, to the person who will read them, who will transmit them. Again and again Gradowski says, "I know you will not believe me. I know, but you must." And then while describing Auschwitz, while describing the disappearance of his community and his family, his children, his wife, at one point he cannot take it any longer. So he says, "I cannot write about this world," and suddenly he writes a 20-page ballad to the moon. His companion, Leib Langfuss, a dayan, a rabbinic judge, wrote his testimony mainly about religious Jews and their agony. Listen. The style is biblical; so is the pace, the rhythm: "We witnessed the arrival of transports from Bendin and Sosnowiec. An elderly rabbi was among them. As they came from nearby towns they knew what was awaiting them. They knew. And the rabbi entered in the undressing room and suddenly he began to dance and to sing all alone. And the others said nothing and he sang and he danced for a long time and then he died for *kiddush ha-shem,* for the sanctification of God's name." Another entry in the same diary by Leib Langfuss: "And the transports began arriving from Hungary and two Jews turned to a member of our commando and asked him whether they should recite the *viddui,* the last confession before dying. And my friend said Yes. So they took a bottle of brandy and drank from it while shouting *l'chaim* to one another with true joy. And they insisted that my friend drink too, but he felt embarrassed, and ashamed. And he said No, but they refused to let him go. They pressed him to drink, to drink and to say *l'chaim* to life, and they said, 'You must live, you must take vengeance. You must. Therefore, we say to you *l'chaim,* to life.' And they kept on repeating *l'chaim, l'chaim,* we understand one another, don't we? *l'chaim.* And my friend drank with them and he was so deeply moved that he began to weep. And he ran out to the place where Jews were being burned and he stayed there several hours and he kept on weeping until at one point he shouted, 'Friends, good friends, you have burned enough.' And he perished in the same flames. Only his words remain."

Who were those men? They were forced to serve the god of fire. They did the burning and they knew their turn would come to be thrown into the flames. Isolated from the rest of the inmates they lived in their own enclosure where, to paraphrase André Malraux, "Man gave lessons to hell." And yet they wrote. I will never know where they found the courage and strength to put one word after another. But they did. You read their tales and often you stop, unable to continue. Gradually you become acquainted with those people. Personally, I found out that the rabbi of my town was taken to be a member of that commando. He was young and strong and he threw himself alive into the flames. You know these people—Loventhal, Gradowski, Langfuss. Some became mad or mute or deeply religious. One started, of all places, there and then to study Talmud. Another collected books of Psalms. All wrote testimony. The way their writings were located and assembled is a story in itself.

Listen to one of the many introductions Zalman Gradowski wrote in Yiddish: "Dear Reader: In these pages you will find an expression of what we, the world's most unfortunate children, endured in a lifetime in the earthly hell named Birkenau-Auschwitz. I believe that the name is by now familiar to the world, but surely no one gives credence to the report on what is taking place here. People may take it as propaganda. So I decided to tell you that what you know, what you may think you know, is but a small fragment of what is really happening.

"This is the place chosen by the enemy to exterminate our people and other peoples as well through gruesome means. And the purpose of my writing is to make sure that at least something of the truth reaches the world and moves it to avenge our lives. This is the purpose of my life."

My good friends, the miracle, the mystery of that experience, one of the mysteries, is that somehow we did not obey their will. Every community, every jail, every cell, every camp reverberated with one order— avenge. Avenge us! Avenge us! And, we did not.

Zalman Gradowski once grimly wrote: "I have a request to you who will discover these pages, a last wish. The wish of a man who knows that his last crossroad is near. We are all doomed. Only the date has not been set as yet. Here is the address of my relatives in New York on East Broadway. Find them, they will know. They will tell you who I am. They have pictures of myself and my family. Publish them together with my testimony. I wish I could think that somewhere someone will shed a tear for me and my family. For I can no longer cry. I drown in a sea of blood. Waves follow one another. Impossible to be alone and cry. Cry over our common tragedy. But I am unable to shed tears and yet at times I feel my soul so wounded, so wounded."

Langfuss writes: "I wish that all my descriptions and notes buried once upon a time and signed 'Jara' may be collected. They can be found in various boxes and jars under the courtyard of Crematorium Two. There are other comprehensive reports, one of them entitled 'The Deportation,' which is inside the grave full of bones near Crematorium One. And a description entitled 'Auschwitz' which is under the leveled bones on the southwestern side of the same courtyard. Later I rewrote and supplemented it and buried it apart among the ashes on the side of Crematorium Two. I wish that all these writings may be published together under the title 'In the Nightmare of Murder.' We are now going to the zone. We are 170 men. We are the last of the commandos. We are being led to die."

Langfuss describes scenes: 200 young Hungarian Jews being beaten savagely before being shot. Emaciated, hungry Jews from Poland who beg members of the *Sonderkommando* to give them bread before being killed. A five-year-old girl undressing her one-year-old brother. Jews from Holland, from Poland. Jews from all over Europe meet in the chambers, and one young woman makes a speech: "We shall not really die here. The history of our people will remember us and make us immortal."

Listen: "This happened to us the end of the summer of 1943. A transport of Jews arrived from Tarnow. They wanted to know where they were being taken. They were told, 'To die.' They were already undressed. They looked grave and silent. Then they began to recite a *viddui.* Then a young Jew stood upon a bench and asked everybody's attention. 'We are not going to die,' he said. And they believed him, and they died."

Listen: "Passover 1944. A transport of important Jews arrived from Vittel, among them Reb Moishe Friedman of Bayone. He undressed together with the others. Suddenly he approached an officer, seized him by the lapels of his uniform, and spoke up. 'You common, cruel murderers. Do not think you will exterminate the Jewish people. The Jewish people will live forever while you murderers will disappear from the world. The day of reckoning is near. Our blood will cry for retribution.' He spoke, and nobody interrupted him. Then he cried out, 'Shema Yisrael (Hear, O Israel),' And all others repeated after him, 'Shema Yisrael.'" Leib Langfuss, who saw it, adds: "Something took hold of all those present. This was an extraordinary, sublime moment, a moment not to be equaled in the lives of men."

In Treblinka there was a man named Yankel Wiernik, a carpenter. During the uprising, together with those who participated in it, he managed to escape and he wrote his story. "Dear reader," he says, "for your sake alone I continue to hang on to my miserable life though it has lost all attraction for me. Time and again I wake up in the middle of the night, moaning pitifully. Phantoms of death haunt me, specters of children, little children. Nothing but children. I sacrificed all those nearest and dearest to me. I myself took them to the place of execution. I built their death chambers for them. And today I am a homeless old man without a roof over my head, without a family, without any next of kin. I talk to myself. I answer my own questions. I am a wanderer. It is with a feeling that all my experiences have become imprinted on my face that I walk. Do I look like a human being? I who saw the doom of three generations must keep on living for the sake of the future. The world must be told of what happened."

Wiernik writes, describing the gas chambers he built, "The machinery of the gas chambers was operated by two Ukrainians. One of them, Ivan, was tall, had kind and gentle eyes, but was nevertheless a sadist. He often attacked us while we worked and nailed our ears to the wall or made us lie down on the floor and whipped us brutally. While doing this his face showed sadistic satisfaction and he laughed and joked. He finished off the gas victims according to his mood. The other mechanic was called Nicholas. I almost went insane on the day when I first saw men, women and children being led into the house of death. I pulled my hair and shed bitter tears of despair. I suffered most when I looked at the children accompanied by their mothers, or walking alone entirely ignorant of the fact that within a few minutes their lives would be snuffed out under horrible torture. Their eyes glowed with fear and still more, perhaps, with amazement. It seemed as if the questions, What is this? What for? and Why? were frozen on their lips." This was a haunting theme for everybody: Why? What's the meaning of all this? Why? For heaven's sake, why? Why so many victims and why so many murders? Why did God allow this to happen? Why do people do this? Why do other people, good people allow this to happen? What is the meaning of all this? Why were factories being built to produce death? Why?

You must listen more. You must listen to more. I repeat, if Wiernik had the courage to write, you must listen.

"Between 450 and 500 persons were crowded into a chamber measuring 125 square feet in Treblinka. Parents carried their children in the vain hope of saving them from death. On the way to their doom they were pushed and beaten with rifle butts and gas pipes. Dogs were set on them, barking, biting and tearing them. It lasted a short while. Then the doors were shut tightly with a bang. Twenty-five minutes later everybody was dead and they stood lifeless; there being no free space, they just leaned against each other. They no longer shouted because the thread of their lives had been broken. They no longer had any needs or desires. Mothers held their children tightly in their arms. There were no more friends, no more enemies. There was no jealousy. All were equal. There was no longer any beauty or ugliness, for all looked yellow from the gas. There were no longer any rich or poor. All were equal. And why all this? That is the question I keep asking myself. My life is hard, very hard. I must live to tell the world about all this."

Another time he says, "Suddenly I saw a live nude woman in the distance. She was young and good-looking, but there was a demented look in her eyes. She said something to us, but we couldn't understand her and were unable to help. She had wrapped herself in a bath sheet, under which she was hiding a little child, and was frantically looking for shelter. Then one of the Germans saw her, ordered her to get into an already dug grave, and shot her and the child dead."

"I am not a young man," says Wiernik, "and I have seen a lot in my lifetime, but Satan himself could not possibly have devised a worse hell. Can you imagine 3,000 corpses recently alive, burning all at once in such an immense fire? Looking at the faces of the dead, one can ordinarily think that they might arise momentarily and awaken from their deep slumber. But here at a given signal they set a giant torch on fire, and it burned with a huge flame."

Why did the Germans do that? Why did they want their victims to be killed a second time? Why did they kill the dead? Why did they burn them? And why did Wiernik describe these burnings? Here is why. Just as the killer was determined to erase Jewish memory, his victims fought to maintain it alive. First the enemy killed the Jews and then he made them disappear in smoke, in ashes, so every Jew was killed twice. In every extermination center special squads of prisoners had to unearth multitudes of corpses and then burn them. Now he tries to kill them for the third time by depriving them of their past, and nothing could be more heinous, more vicious than that. I repeat, nothing is or could be as ugly, as inhuman as the wish to deprive the dead victims of their death. Hence our profound conviction. Anyone who does not actively, constantly engage in remembering and in making others remember is an accomplice of the enemy. Conversely, whoever opposes the enemy must take the side of his victims and communicate their tales, tales of solitude and despair, tales of silence and defiance.

In a train going to Treblinka a woman wrote a letter to the world and entrusted it to the wind. In a bunker in a Polish ghetto a girl composed a poem and wrote the words in the invisible sky. In an attic in Wilno an old sage recited *kaddish* all alone, wondering whether anyone was listening, whether anyone cared. To be remembered, that was all they wanted. They did not want to be helped anymore—they knew they were beyond help—but they wanted to be remembered. Their names, their faces, their songs, their secrets. Their struggle and their death. One as awesome as the other. Not to be forgotten. Hundreds and thousands of men and women joined in conspiracy, often as a self-sacrifice, to enable one messenger to get out and deliver one message, always the same, to the outside world. To bear witness.

The armed rebellions in various ghettos, the uprisings in Sobibor, Chelmno, Treblinka, Birkenau were motivated by that urge. To inform, to alert, to indict, to add to the history of our people one more chapter, the most terrifying of all. It was not easy to remember. It is not easy to remember. It was not easy to relive those days and those nights and not go insane. It was not easy to be with those children and go on living, praying, singing. It was not and is not easy to return to those nocturnal processions. There was something solemn about the way they converged over there, something mystical, all those men and women and children, families and strangers, friends and relatives walking, walking with the same steady gaze in their burning eyes. They did not cry nor did they shout, nor did they ask pity or compassion. They walked quietly, not ever looking back. And so numerous were they that they suggested the infinite. One had the impression that they would go on walking, walking forever, until the end of time.

A father talks to his son, explaining something, and we shall never know what it was. "Does it hurt to die?" asks a child. "No," says the mother, "it does not." As a Jew, I am confronted with that mystery and I cannot close my eyes to it. Whatever I see, I see through that event. But, again, it would be wrong to assume that it means something only to us Jews. It means to mankind that whatever happens to us may happen to everybody. And furthermore, forgive me—I am going to say something harsh; I do not mean to use it in order to divide us, but, on the contrary, to try to bring us closer to another. But a truth must be said. If the victims are my problem the killers are not. The killers are someone else's problem, not mine.

If I want to understand, and never will, why my people turned into victims, into perfect victims, somebody will have to understand or try to understand why all the killers were Christians, bad Christians surely, but Christians. Somebody will have to explain why so many killers were intellectuals, academicians, college professors, lawyers, engineers, physicians, theologians. The *Einsatzkommandos,* those who did the killing directly, not in the gas chambers, were led by intellectuals. They were not shielded by their culture. They proved that knowledge without morality may be destructive, that science alone without ethical dimension may become an instrument of inhumanity.

As for myself, I do not know. The boy that began to talk to you tonight, where is he? Did he dream or live his dreams of fear and fire? Did he really witness the agony of mankind, through the death of his community? Did he really see the triumph of brutality, did he hear or imagine the laughter of the executioner? Did he really see killers throwing children, Jewish children, into the flames alive? I rarely speak about this; but in this place we must. For a very long while I resisted accepting this story as mine. For years and years I clung to the belief that it was all a dream, a nightmare. No, I did not see the children. I did not see the flames.

It was no dream. It was real. Jewish children, living Jewish children were thrown into the flames in order to save money because the gas was costly. What are we to do with this truth that they brought back from there? What are we to do with the knowledge accumulated over there? In all of us there existed one fear and one alone, to be the last, the last witness, the last messenger, the last to remember, the last to know. Should he or she die, the enemy will have achieved their victory. Nothing then would remain of what has taken place over there.

I have tried to describe these obsessions in one of my novels. A central character is the last survivor, the one who cannot die. The entire community has been killed, and only one person remains, the young *yeshiva bochur,* a student. And the killer shoots, he fires his gun into him, he fires all the shots into him, and the boy cannot die. So the officer is filled with rage, and he says to him, "You think that you'll be happy? You'll not be. You will curse me for sparing you because you will be the last. You think that you have the truth, but your truth is the truth of a madman."

Let me return to the beginning. If we are to believe all those morally deranged persons, then the Holocaust never took place. The killers did not kill, the victims did not perish. Auschwitz was a fraud, Treblinka a lie, Bergen-Belsen a convalescent home. What does one say to such persons, and why haven't more people spoken out? Some of the survivors and many of the executioners are still in our midst. Suddenly I understand why, during the Auschwitz trial in Frankfurt, all the defendants, the killers of Auschwitz, came day after day into court laughing, laughing. They knew why. Ghetto fighters from Warsaw and Bialystok, you have not witnessed the death of your families. Survivors of Sobibor and Ponar, you have not lost your parents to the flames. Chelmno and Majdanek, Belzec, and Janowska are not places where entire communities were reduced to ashes. Ringelblum and Kaplan wrote nothing. Yankel Wiernik's report meant nothing. The Nuremberg trials, the *Einsatzkommando* trials, the Frankfurt trials were never held. Höss was just another officer and Eichmann a bureaucrat. There was no uprising in Treblinka and no selection in Birkenau. But then, you may ask, where have the people disappeared? Where are the three million Polish Jews? Where are the one million Hungarian Jews? What happened to the Jews of my town? What happened to the other *shtetlach,* the other towns in Hungary, Estonia, Lithuania, Greece, Holland and the Ukraine? Where are more than one million Jewish children? Are they hiding? If there was no Holocaust, where have they vanished? There are in this audience fellow survivors. Think about these questions. For soon you may have to answer them. Soon you may be held responsible if not for the Holocaust then at least for the myth of the Holocaust. Obscene, this attempt to deprive the victim of his memories. It is not new. Your colleague here cannot even boast of having invented something. The diary of Anne Frank was only recently termed a forgery by an ambassador at the United Nations. A prominent European playwright wrote a play about the Auschwitz trials and managed not to mention the word "Jew" therein, not once. We find no monument for Jewish victims at Babi Yar, as there is none in Auschwitz. A former SS judge wrote a book in Germany and he says, "Not a single Jew was killed in Auschwitz. I was there as a judge of the SS. Yes, there were chimneys but the chimneys were bakeries."

Gerhardt Frey, the leader of the SS today in Germany, recently told a convention that the Holocaust was a lie, a hoax of the century. I confess I do not know how to handle this situation. Are we really to debate these ideas or charges? Is it not beneath our dignity and the dignity of the dead even to refute those lies? But then, is silence the answer? It never was. And that is why we try to tell the tale. But what are the messengers of the dead to do with their memories? They would much rather speak about other things. But who then would protest against the recent attempts to kill the victims again? There was no Treblinka. There was no Buchenwald. And we were not there, fellow survivors. I do not know how you react to all this. I can only tell you what one survivor feels. More than sadness, he feels dismay, and more than dismay he feels despair, and even more than despair, he feels disgust.

In conclusion, a Hasidic story. And it came to pass that a traveler lost his way in the forest. He walked and walked day and night, all by himself, full of fear and crushed by fatigue. And suddenly he saw a castle and was overcome with joy. Then he saw that the castle was burning and he was overcome with sadness. It must be an empty castle, thought the wanderer. But then he heard a voice crying, "Help me, help me. I am the owner of the castle." And the solitary Rebbe of Kotsk, who quoted this midrashic tale, pounded the table with his fist shouting, "The castle is ablaze, the wanderer is lost, the forest is burning, but the owner is calling for help. What does it mean? It means that there is an owner." As for us, we would paraphrase the story and say, "The castle is ablaze, the wanderer is lost, the forest is burning, the entire world is burning and we are still inside, inside the burning castle."

Lucy S. Dawidowicz

Historian and author, Lucy S. Dawidowicz is professor of social history at Yeshiva University in New York, where she holds the Eli and Diana Zborowski Professorial Chair in Interdisciplinary Holocaust Studies. She received a Guggenheim fellowship in 1976 and currently is working on a history of Jews in America.

A native New Yorker, Professor Dawidowicz studied at Hunter College, Columbia University and the Yivo Institute for Jewish Research. She is the author of *The War Against the Jews 1933-1945,* published in 1975. The volume was awarded an Anisfield-Wolf prize. A companion volume which she edited, *A Holocaust Reader,* followed a year later. Her latest book, published in 1977, is *The Jewish Presence: Essays on Identity and History.*

Professor Dawidowicz also is the author of *The Golden Tradition: Jewish Life and Thought in Eastern Europe* and co-author with Leon J. Goldstein of *Politics in a Pluralist Democracy.*

THE HOLOCAUST
AS HISTORICAL RECORD

by Lucy S. Dawidowicz

On October 4, 1943, Heinrich Himmler, Reichsführer-SS, the head of the most dreaded police force in all Europe, addressed a meeting of top SS officers in Poznan. It was a time when Germany was under severe military pressure, driven inexorably by the Russians to retreat; a time when Anglo-American bombings were crippling German war industry, when the Allies had incontestably established their land and air superiority. Himmler, holding forth before his SS officers, no doubt intended to bolster their morale. He expatiated on his beloved Führer, on the nobility of the SS, on the grandeur of German culture, on the sanctity of German blood. And on the murder of the Jews. That was a time also when the German dictatorship had already murdered five million Jews. This is what Himmler said:

"I also want to make reference before you here, in complete frankness, to a really grave matter. Among ourselves, this once, it shall be uttered quite frankly; but in public we will never speak of it . . . I am referring to the evacuation of the Jews, the annihilation of the Jewish people . . . Most of you must know what it means to see a hundred corpses lie side by side, or five hundred, or a thousand. To have stuck this out and . . . to have kept our integrity, this is what has made us hard. In our history, this is an unwritten and never-to-be-written page of glory."

The text of Himmler's speech eventually found its way into SS files. In 1945, those files, along with countless other official records of the German dictatorship, its government archives, diplomatic reports, institutional files, memoranda and minutes, fell into the hands of the victorious Allies. The Western Allies—the United States, England, and France—agreed from the start to make these captured German documents available to the scholarly community. Never before had historians had such a total and unhindered access to the official records of a state. In fact, the superabundance of captured German documents has presented to the historian a problem nearly as severe and crippling as the lack of documentation altogether, since the behemoth proportions of these seized papers conspire against man's frailty and the limits of his time. (Descriptions of the documentary sources dealing with the murder of the Jews are drawn from the introduction to my book, *A Holocaust Reader,* Behrman House, New York, 1976.)

The captured German documents comprise the records of federal, regional, and local government agencies, of military commands and units, as well as of the National Socialist Party, covering a period ranging from 1920 to 1945. After the war they were brought to the United States and housed in a depot at Alexandria, Va., where they were sorted, classified, and microfilmed. They have since been returned to the Federal Republic of Germany. Sixty-seven *Guides to German Records Microfilmed at Alexandria, Va.,* prepared under the direction of the Committee for the Study of War Documents of the American Historical Association, have been published by the National Archives, comprising about 7,500 pages. An average page in a guide covers almost 2,000 frames of film, which means that the captured German documents now available on microfilm from the National Archives total about fifteen million pages.

From the outset, the Allied powers as well as all liberated countries where masses of German documents were seized regarded the German records primarily as legal evidence and documentary proof to be used at the trials of German war criminals. Operating under the exigencies of time, army intelligence personnel, translators, lawyers, scholars, and specialists began to sift the mountainous accumulations of documents for this purpose. The United States teams alone examined about 100,000 documents individually, designating about 40,000 as valuable. These were then subjected to rigorous screening to search out the most persuasive evidence of war crimes and crimes against humanity committed by the Germans. The documents finally selected became the exhibits presented by the American prosecution at the trial of the twenty-two major war criminals held before the International Military Tribunal at Nuremberg. Great Britain, France, and the Soviet Union, each with its own storehouse of seized German documents, similarly developed exhibits and evidence.

The trial proceedings and the documents admitted in evidence were published—in identical English, French, and German versions—in forty-two volumes, known as the "Blue Series." The United States published its documents under the title *Nazi Conspiracy and Aggression,* in eight volumes and supplements, the "Red Series"; documents not introduced or admitted as evidence were included there.

After the trial of the major war criminals, there were twelve subsequent proceedings before Nuremberg military tribunals in which implicated Germans were tried for a wide range of crimes, including medical crimes, the murders committed by the Einsatzgruppen, the complicity of state ministries and armed services in war crimes, and the participation of industrialists in the exploitation of slave labor. A condensed record and selected documents were published in fifteen volumes, the "Green Series." Himmler's speech, from which I quoted, was one of the thousands of documents selected for use as evidence by American staff working under the direction of Colonel Robert G. Storey, Chief of the Documentation Division of the Office of United States Chief of Counsel for the Prosecution of Axis Criminology. This particular document can be found in the Blue, the Green and the Red Series.

No one can guess what proportion of the mammoth accumulation of German records refers to the Jews, though clearly the amount must be substantial. Every agency of the German state and of the National Socialist Party was involved in one way or another, at one time or another, in anti-Jewish activities, and that involvement was recorded in files, letters, minutes of meetings, reports, memoranda, directives, legislation, speeches, proceedings of conferences, summaries of interdepartmental negotiations, bulletins, statistics, and daily logs. Of the documents brought in evidence at the thirteen trials at Nuremberg, which comprise a very small proportion of all the captured German records, about 3,000 deal with the Jews, their persecution, expropriation, and annihilation.

The Jewish records of the Holocaust, the documents which provide the foundation for the history of Jewish endurance and suffering, differ altogether in dimension and character from the captured German records. The Jewish documents are far fewer in number and, in contrast to most archival sources, contain a larger proportion of personal papers than of official records. European Jews had no government and no state archives. Under German persecution, even the *Judenräte*—Jewish councils—the only official institutions in the ghettos, maintained records with caution and discretion. Indeed, everywhere among Jews under German occupation, care and circumspection determined what and how much was committed to paper. Nevertheless, the Jews in the ghettos were resolute in their determination to leave a documentary record for posterity, even if they themselves did not expect to survive.

In a collective undertaking without historical parallel, East European Jews generated massive archives, and even arranged for their preservation so that evidence might remain of their ordeals and sufferings. All over Europe and especially in Poland, the Jews conspired against their perse-

cutors to keep a historical and documentary record, though the very existence of such a record jeopardized both writer and collector, historian and
archivist. That much of this material survived the destruction of the war
which the Germans waged against the Jews was not accidental, but was
the consequence of conscious Jewish design and policy. The ghetto Jews
worked out techniques for safeguarding their documents until after the war
and the defeat of the Germans. Some records were buried underground;
others were hidden in secure and protected places; still others were transmitted to trustworthy non-Jews. The actual survival of these records was
guaranteed, then, by the preparations and sacrificial efforts of the Jews
themselves.

The most celebrated of Jewish communal archives was the Oneg
Shabbat ("Pleasures of the Sabbath"), the code name which historian
Emmanuel Ringelblum gave to his conspiratorial undertaking to document
Jewish experiences under the German occupation and to preserve a record
of the cataclysmic transformations which the whole Jewish settlement in
Poland was undergoing.

As early as October 1939, in the first weeks of the German occupation of Warsaw, Ringelblum began to keep daily notes of events. From
his vantage point in a self-help welfare organization, he gathered information brought by friends and clients. Local people reported developments
in Warsaw and visitors told of events in outlying areas. Refugees and
delegations seeking aid for their uprooted communities came from hundreds of towns and cities throughout German-occupied Poland and brought
first-hand news about what had happened to them.

At first unsuccessful in involving others in this enterprise, Ringelblum
concluded that a more organized effort was needed. In May 1940 he gathered a small group of colleagues to engage in such a collective undertaking. Because the group met on Saturdays, it chose the name Oneg Shabbat as a cover for its activities. Secretary of the association was Hersh
Wasser, a refugee from Lodz, whose involvement in welfare work brought
him into contact with hundreds of refugees and expelled Jews from all
over Poland. He initiated a project to gather monographic accounts of the
fate of their communities; indeed, a considerable number of such studies,
describing the impact of the war and the German occupation upon Polish
villages, towns and cities, were written by direct participants, with first-
hand knowledge of the events.

After November 1940, when Warsaw Jews were imprisoned within the
ghetto, Oneg Shabbat expanded its activities. A master plan was elabo-
rated for documentation and research and assignments were given out to

reliable persons who for the most part were not trained as historians or journalists. Their reliability was with regard to confidentiality in the collection of material. Gathering and writing such documents were, according to the German occupiers, criminal acts, punishable by death. Everything that happened to the Jews in Poland was grist for the mill, to be written down, systematized, analyzed. Eventually Ringelblum hoped to use the materials for historical studies and as legal evidence against the Germans. German atrocities, economic conditions, the structure of ghetto institutions, youth activities, forced-labor camps, experiences in prisons and concentration camps, religious life, ghetto folklore (poems, jokes, curses, sayings)—all this and much more fell within the ambitious scope of Oneg Shabbat. Staff members accumulated official German, Polish, and Jewish documents. Copies of the underground Jewish and Polish press were kept, at great risk. Letters sent to Warsaw from all over Poland were collected in the thousands, as a rich source of information about local communities. Influential figures in the Jewish community were interviewed, to preserve for the record their ideas on the impact of the ghetto on Jewish morality and morale.

Above all, the ghetto Jews were encouraged to keep diaries, to record the daily events of their existence. To stimulate such activity, Oneg Shabbat, using the cover of the local welfare agency, sponsored contests, offering cash prizes. One Oneg Shabbat worker set down his views on this enterprise:

"I regard it as a sacred task . . . for everyone, whether or not he has the ability, to write down everything that he has witnessed or has heard from those who witnessed the atrocities which the barbarians committed in every Jewish town. When the time will come—and indeed it will surely come—let the world read and know what the murderers perpetrated. This will be the richest material for the mourner when he writes the elegy for the present time. This will be the most powerful subject matter for the avenger . . . We are obligated to assist them, to help them, even if we must pay with our own lives, which today are very cheap."

The sense of dedication and sacrificial commitment motivated everyone associated with Oneg Shabbat, regardless of his specific task. A nineteen-year-old youth described his feelings on concealing archives in an underground hiding place in August 1942, at the time of the mass deportations from the Warsaw ghetto to the death camp at Treblinka:

"My work was primitive, consisting of packing and hiding the material . . . It was perhaps the riskiest, but it was worth doing. We used to say while working: 'We can die in peace. We have bequeathed and safeguarded our rich heritage.' I don't want any thanks. It will be enough for me if the coming generations will recall our times. We were aware of our obligation. We did not fear the risk. We reckoned that we were creating a chapter of history and that was more important than several lives. I can say with assurance that this was the basis, the dynamic of our existence then. What we could not cry out to the world, we buried in the ground. May this treasure be delivered into good hands, may it live to see better times, so that it can alert the world to what happened in the twentieth century."

After the war, substantial portions of the Oneg Shabbat archives were located and recovered.

Ringelblum's Oneg Shabbat served as a model for the Jews in the Bialystok ghetto. The Bialystok archives, initiated by Mordecai Tenenbaum who had come from Warsaw in November 1942 to organize the resistance movement, enjoyed the support of Ephraim Barash, head of the Bialystok Judenrat, and consequently included most of the minutes, proclamations, reports, and other official documents of the Judenrat and its institutions. In addition, a systematic effort was made to gather eyewitness reports and journalistic and historical accounts of the war, the Soviet occupation from 1939 to 1941, and the subsequent German occupation. Ghetto folklore and poetry and the records of the underground Zionist youth movement enriched the collection. In the spring of 1943, when the ghetto's continued existence hung in the balance, arrangements were made to have the archives buried in a secure place outside the ghetto. Three metal boxes were constructed and filled with documents, and were then hermetically sealed to protect them from decay. By May 1943, the boxes were clandestinely transferred out of the ghetto and buried. They were found after the war.

In the Vilna ghetto, a team of writers and intellectuals conspired to create an archive of official Judenrat documents as well as to stimulate people to keep diaries. They even succeeded in removing manuscripts and rare books from the renowned library of the Yiddish Scientific Institute (YIVO), which the Germans had impounded. All these materials, the old and the new, were hidden first from the Germans and then, after the German retreat from Vilna, from the Soviet authorities. Eventually, at great personal risk, two Yiddish poets who had organized the whole undertaking, Shmerke Kaczerginsky and Abraham Sutzkever, managed to send about 700 ghetto documents and some prewar materials to the YIVO in New York through clandestine channels.

The most extraordinary archive ever created was buried at Auschwitz. It consisted of eyewitness testimonies written by members of the *Sonderkommando* ("special commando"), a work squad of Jewish prisoners whom the Germans had temporarily spared from the gas chambers. Their task was to remove the dead from the gas chambers and cremate them. In due time the members of the *Sonderkommando* were themselves gassed and replaced by new workers. In the full realization that they would not survive, some members of the *Sonderkommando,* under conditions of extreme peril, wrote accounts of the events they had witnessed. They buried their records in the ashes that covered the ground at Auschwitz. These were found after the war, in bad condition, some scarcely decipherable.

One testimony began: "Dear finder, search everywhere, in every inch of ground. Dozens of documents are buried beneath it, mine and those of other persons, which will throw light on everything that happened here. Great quantities of teeth also are buried here. It was we, the commando workers, who deliberately strewed them all over the ground, as many as we could, so that the world should find material traces of the millions of murdered people. We ourselves have lost hope of being able to live to see the moment of liberation."

Most of these Jewish records, buried in, and later exhumed from, Polish soil, remained in Poland, where they formed the core of the documentary collections of the Jewish Historical Institute in Warsaw, the central repository in Poland of Holocaust archives. Though that material has not been readily available to foreign scholars, much of it has been duplicated and is available, along with countless other records, in the archives of the Yad Vashem, the Martyrs' and Heroes' Memorial Authority, in Jerusalem, in the archives of the YIVO Institute for Jewish Research in New York, and in other repositories in Israel and Europe.

These documents—the captured German documents as well as the surviving Jewish documents—have been the raw materials with which the scholars have worked in studying the Nazi era. The scholarly literature of this event-laden twelve-year period has grown to immense proportions. The rise and fall of the German dictatorship and especially of its dictator continue to fascinate scholars and the public at large. Yet the history of the Holocaust, the annihilation of six million European Jews by that dictatorship, has occupied a relatively small place in modern scholarship. The exceptions, predictable of course, are the works of contemporary German and contemporary Jewish scholars. The German historians—and I speak of the generation which came to maturity after the Second World War—are in search of moral wholeness and wish to confront their national past, the history of their parents and their people. The Jewish scholars, for their part, have assimilated the history of the Nazi persecutions into the framework of millennial Jewish history, in which persecution and suffering recur with implacable persistence.

In this country it appears that the Holocaust as the subject for research and study has been relegated largely to Jewish scholars, as if it were a matter of narrow parochial interest. After all, the Holocaust appeared to have left no visible effects, no tangible results in the world, except for its terrible impact on the Jews. A millennium of Jewish history came to an end in the slaughter of the six million. The East European wellsprings of Jewish creativity, both traditional and modern, which for generations had nourished Jewish communities throughout the world were stopped up. The Holocaust changed the course of Jewish history. Because of the six million Israel received its original political legitimation and the face of the Jews as a people was radically transformed.

But the Jewish perspective does not define the world we live in. Rosa Luxemburg, a Jew who spoke for the world, once wrote to a friend who lived with a Jewish perspective: "Why do you come with your special Jewish sorrows? I feel just as sorry for the wretched Indian victims in Putamayo, for the Negroes in Africa." The Holocaust, it would appear, has become only a "special Jewish sorrow," for those Jews who live with a Jewish perspective, not even for those Jews who share Rosa Luxemburg's perspective. To be sure, the initial encounter with the murder of the six million shook and shocked the whole world—that is, the gentile bystanders. But the observer's shock, if not internalized, wears off. And it has worn off.

The historians no doubt argue that other events of this century were far more noteworthy—the Russian Revolution, the rise of Communist China as a world power, the emergence of the Third World, the wonderful and terrible achievements of modern science and technology. Yet in ways perhaps invisible and intangible, the Holocaust has profoundly affected the course of Western civilization.

At the mention of the German name of an obscure Polish village, Auschwitz, our familiar quotidian world, inhabited by family and friends, enriched by work and books, informed by pleasure and beauty, disintegrates. Surely the perimeters of the Holocaust have defined the universe of evil and of good, have marked the limits of human bestiality and human arrogance, set the measure for human endurance and courage. The Holocaust tested man and God. Professor Roy Eckhardt has described the Holocaust as "*metanoia,* the climactic turning-around of the entire world," when the history of man and of God "comes up to a fatal watershed."

But this is the language of metahistory. The Holocaust was a real historical event, in real time, in our own lifetime; in real space marked in every child's geography book. Why has it found so little place in the history books? Why has it had so little resonance in contemporary thought?

Three reasons can explain the meager treatment of the Holocaust in the histories and textbooks. The first is the historian's perception of the Jew. The second is his view of human history and of historiography; the third is his attitude toward Germany and the Germans.

The "egocentric predicament," a term which philosopher Ralph Barton Perry used to describe the inability of men to see the world except through their own eyes, can serve as the most charitable explanation as to why Jews, Judaism, and Jewish culture occupy so small a space in modern history and philosophy. Jews, after all, belong to a minority people and history—world history, national history—is written *by* the majority *about* the majority, *for* the majority. Professor Gavin Langmuir of Stanford first coined the phrase "majority history" some years back in a penetrating study of the treatment or, more precisely, nontreatment and mistreatment, of Jews in post-Biblical European history.

The rise of the Christian Church and its subsequent triumph over Judaism put the Jews outside history thereafter. The Jewish past was rewritten in the light of Christian doctrine and for centuries the very existence of the Jews was determined by that doctrine. During the hegemony of the Church in medieval Europe, the Jews remained for the most part the outsiders, at times tolerated, at times persecuted, unassimilable in Christian society. With the rise of the nation-states, the Jews continued to remain outsiders, sometimes tolerated, but often persecuted because they were regarded as alien to the developing national ethos. Eventually they became the mortal victims of overdeveloped nationalism. Since history in modern times has largely been the handmaiden of the state, it is not surprising then that Jewish history should have received so little regard and that the presence of the Jews in the world should have been unnoticed by the historians, except for occasional outbursts that reflected the historian's nationalist bias rather than his objective professional assessment. Since what happens to the Jews is considered Jewish history, the Holocaust is relegated to Jewish history and consequently is regarded as of little moment to the American or Englishman or Frenchman. This outlook largely accounts for the sorry fact that the Holocaust is so inadequately recorded in the histories and texts used in our colleges and schools.

The second factor to explain why the Holocaust receives such niggardly treatment in contemporary history is the historian's rationalist bias. In writing history, the historian seeks explanations for the events which he describes and analyzes. He looks for cause and effect, motive and goal. The course of history, the rise and fall of nations and civilizations, is studied scientifically, dissected by examining political events, economic developments, social determinants. History—that is, historical writing—is a rationalist enterprise which searches out meaning and sometimes purpose in the progression of events. Historians have been singularly indifferent—or is it insensitive?—to the irrational, whether as cause or effect. The history of mass psychopathology is still to be written: the history of mass delusions and popular crazes, of cycles of mass hysteria which intersect those more conventional types of history—diplomatic history, political history, the history of ideas, social history. To be sure, with the emergence in the last decade or so of psychohistory, a discipline which attempts to penetrate the darker mysteries of the character and personality of historical movers and shakers, more consideration is being given to irrational factors in political and social history. But generally, except for a handful of first-rate scholars and thinkers, the place, the function, and the operation of mass psychopathology in human history have been ignored and neglected. Death, the family, sexual behavior, violence have today become legitimated as subjects of historical inquiry. Yet only a bare handful of historians are engaged in studying historical phenomena of mass hysteria and sociopathology—the witch crazes, religious persecution, anti-Semitism, mass political paranoia.

Is it because historians are uncomfortable with the basic, underlying irrationality which they must confront in such study? Is it that they suffer from what Professor Gershom Scholem, that extraordinary historian of Jewish mysticism, characterized as the "rationalist perversion of sound judgment"?

The derangements of anti-Semitism and the frenzy of racism embarrass and confound the historian. Most historians—again there are notable exceptions—approach the study of anti-Semitism with a rationalist perspective, looking for reasons and explanations for the phenomenon of anti-Semitism, not in the obsessions of the anti-Semites, but in the behavior of the Jews or in the impersonal processes of history—economic cycles of prosperity and depression, capitalism, imperialism. Even Jewish historians, the most rationalist of historians, minutely study the Jews to find flaws in them so that they can produce a rational rationale for anti-Semitism! Alas, they do not understand the chameleon-like versatility of anti-Semitism; they have not grasped its protean character, that it will transform itself, its theses and hypotheses, its specific targets and objections according to whatever the Jews are at any moment in history. In the course of their history, Jews have been persecuted for believing in Judaism and excoriated for disbelieving; despised when poor and loathed when rich; shamed for their ignorance of the host culture and rebuffed for mastering it; denounced as capitalists and assailed as Communists, derided for their separatism and reviled for their assimilationism. Whatever the Jews are or do at any particular time in history—the very nature of their existence—feeds the animus of the Jew-hater and consequently serves as the "explanation" for hating the Jews.

Thirdly, we come to the problem of the historian's attitude toward Germany. Sooner or later the historian must confront the question of National Socialism and its place in German history. Did it represent a continuity of German political traditions and culture or was it an aberration? The idea of National Socialism as an aberration, as a deviation from the expected trajectory of German history, is more palatable to scholars who have emotional ties to their subject matter but offers little moral comfort or political reassurance. If the historian sees National Socialism merely as an aberration, a freakish excrescence, he then reveals the Germans as a people and nation too weak and susceptible to strange diseases, unable to offer political resistance to itinerant drummers who mislead them. Little wonder that German historians have an enormous emotional burden in writing the history of their recent past; little wonder that defining the "German Question" becomes a matter of crucial significance. In its most commonly stated form, the German Question is: "How was National Socialism possible?" In its least articulated form, it is: "How was Auschwitz possible?" The question confronts the German historian with the *unbewältigte Vergangenheit,* the unmastered past. It is the problem of coming to terms with a morally repellent and degrading history.

The answers to the German Question range over the historical, political, and moral gamut, from those whose consciencelessness still commits them to a defense of Nazism to those who are not afraid to explore Germany's Nazi past with open eyes. The extreme case is illustrated by a handful of neo-Nazi pseudohistorians, little more than propagandists, still loyal to National Socialism, still hating the Jews, who, since the 1950s, have continued to deny the criminal acts of the Nazi past, which of course they approve and applaud. That process of denial is guilt reduction with a vengeance. They keep their beliefs at the price of their moral integrity and their mental health. In contemporary Germany, these persistent Nazis, if they are professionals, are disciplined by their peers and even sentenced by the courts for incitement of hatred of Jews.

German historians who have not suppressed the question have answered it in a variety of ways, sometimes touching on German anti-Semitism diffidently, gingerly, sometimes with a curious neutrality. The older generation of German scholars, in trying to explain to their students what had happened, have engaged in something of a "national apologia." The younger generations of German historians are far more likely to approach the question of Germany's National Socialist past with intellectual integrity and indeed with humane morality. Pride of place surely belongs to Professor Karl Dietrich Bracher, whose book *The German Dictatorship,* a superb work of historical synthesis, places German anti-Semitism and the consequent annihilation of the Jews in the very center of the historical action.

Having given you a capsule explanation for the inadequate treatment of the Holocaust by the historians, let me now ask: Does it matter that the Holocaust has not been given its proper place in history? No doubt the history books are silent also about other chapters in human history. Not all historical work, it may be argued, can do justice to every horror, to every aberration, to every catastrophe.

I believe that there is a difference between the Holocaust—the word with the capital "H" to designate the destruction of European Jews—and other cataclysmic events in history. In every case of terrible human destructiveness that we have known, even in the most hated war in which Americans participated, killing was not an end in itself, but a means to an end, even though perpetrators, victims, and bystanders differed on whether those ends were good or evil. (Consider the problem which theologians and politicians must sometimes confront—the just war.) But in the murder of the European Jews, ends and means were identical. The German dictatorship murdered the Jews for the purpose of murdering the Jews. For the Germans arrogated to themselves the decision as to who was entitled to live on this earth and who was not. That is the uniqueness of the Holocaust.

For those who ponder these matters, the Holocaust has altered our historical consciousness. We have seen what man can do. Things once inconceivable are now not only possible but actual. In 1897, when the Dreyfus Affaire was tearing France apart, Bernard Lazare, a French Jew active in Dreyfus's defense, addressed a group of Jewish students in Paris on the subject of anti-Semitism. "For the Christian peoples," he remarked, "an Armenian solution to their Jew-hatred was available." He was referring to the Turkish decimation of the Armenian people, a monstrous historical event that bears comparison with the murder of the Jews. But, Lazare went on, "their sensibilities cannot allow them to envisage that." Fifty years later, few Christian sensibilities were aroused by the murder of the Jews. Perhaps that was why a prominent Protestant theologian characterized the Holocaust as "a Christian catastrophe."

Historically and morally the Holocaust is not just a Jewish parochial matter. It is a subject of urgency to the entire community of men. "Unwillingness to know, forgetfulness and even disbelief"—here lies the danger, said the German philosopher Karl Jaspers. What men do today becomes the source of their future actions. Therefore we must know. Let me close by quoting once more from Karl Jaspers: "That which has happened is a warning. To forget it is guilt. It must be continually remembered. It was possible for this to happen, and it remains possible for it to happen again at any minute. Only in knowledge can it be prevented."

Dorothy Rabinowitz

For Jews, says author Dorothy Rabinowitz, the Holocaust is at the center of consciousness.

"If you grew up in the shadow of World War II and the Final Solution, a day doesn't pass without thinking of the Holocaust," she says. The thoughts led to a book, *New Lives: Survivors of the Holocaust Living in America,* a record of those who witnessed and lived to bear witness.

Traveling across the country, Ms. Rabinowitz sought out those who lived through the concentration camps and emigrated to the United States. The result is a collection of remarkable portraits.

Born in New York, Ms. Rabinowitz attended Queens College and New York University's Graduate School of Arts and Sciences. She has lectured in English at New York University and the State University of New York at Stony Brook. In 1973 she received a senior fellowship from the National Endowment for the Humanities. In 1976 the New York Society of Clinical Psychologists bestowed on her its Holocaust Memorial Award.

THE HOLOCAUST AS LIVING MEMORY

by Dorothy Rabinowitz

In the winter of 1973 in New York City, deportation hearings were held for Hermine Braunsteiner Ryan, wife of an American citizen, a resident of Queens, New York. Former SS guard at Ravensbrueck and Majdanek, Mrs. Ryan stood accused of beating inmates to death during the years 1939-1944 while performing her role as vice-commandant of the women's camp at Majdanek; of being responsible, also, for the death selection of hundreds of others. A stream of witnesses arrived at the small hearing room of the Immigration and Naturalization Service headquarters to give evidence. These were former prisoners at Majdanek. The witnesses were restrained, inscrutable in manner, obedient to all the rules of conduct, the civilized assumptions of that society of which they were a part, twenty-eight years after their liberation. They had learned, among other things, that in this society a show of vengeance or any talk of it would be a form of behavior strictly to be avoided. They had learned when questioned by reporters or on the witness stand to say that they were not interested in vengeance: justice, only justice was their concern. This denial of vengeance, these prohibitions were nothing new for them and so were not difficult postures for the survivors to assume. What was required of them in the courtroom was what had regularly been required of them in their old lives, it seemed. They had understood early on that they must be brief and sparing in their testimony about the past, their attestations of things seen and endured between the years 1939 and 1945; about the obliteration not alone of their own families, roots, ties, holdings, homes and livelihoods but of an entire universe. Therefore they were prepared for the fact that the testimony they could give about Majdanek would be limited, confined only to relevant comments, evidence. So in the courtroom that winter in 1973 witness after witness arrived and gave himself over quite willingly to the complexities of justice and due process, there being in the world no more ardent devotees of the democratic procedure than these particular citizens of the United States. The judge directed them to be precise, to avoid outbursts and emotionalism, understandable as such feelings might be. And they did avoid these things, although some survivors of Majdanek wore cloudy, resigned looks upon their faces upon hearing the questions Mrs. Braunsteiner's attorney asked. Such strange questions: "Why," he had asked one witness, why when the SS beat two women prisoners to death did the other prisoners not rush over to help?" Questions also such as what hour and what dates events took place in the camp. The witnesses answered as best they could, knowing that such questions were proper in a courtroom. They answered that in the death camp there were no watches, no calendars. As to why they did not rush forward to intercede to help the women whom Mrs. Braunsteiner had whipped to death they had no immediate available answer to give. Silence. Mrs. Braunsteiner's attorney put this question to one survivor witness over and over: There had been forty or more prisoners at Majdanek, watching; how could it be during these beatings that they just stood by? Silence again. The attorney asked his question once more: "You mean there were forty or more of you, you all had shovels and you didn't stop the beatings? You all just stood and watched?" The witness answered finally, "What do you mean? I don't understand you." But of course this was not so. The witness, like the other survivors, understood well enough that the intent of such questions was to suggest that Majdanek was a place like any other in the world, housing a society like any other, composed of people who could choose between one form of behavior and another, could choose to save their fellows if only they *would.* It was not, of course, the first time the survivors had heard assumptions like these about the abyss that they had endured. Rather, it was the first time they had encountered the willful perversion of history in a courtroom or in any of the American institutions from which they had come to expect rectitude, truth, propriety. Whatever innocent or deliberate untruths about the Holocaust they had got used to hearing in that world of ordinary citizens in whose midst they lived they had, they thought, reason to expect a regard for the facts of history in a courtroom, even from the mouth of a hostile defense attorney. But this was not necessarily true, they discovered; they found it possible in 1973 to hear Ravensbrueck described by the defense attorney as a rehabilitation camp whose purpose was to reeducate the prisoners. They found that it was possible to hear the facts of history denied in a courtroom, that this refusal of the facts of history would be heard without much objection, and treated as though it were an argument as good as any other. It was the first time they had heard such things, but it would not be the last. They would, like the rest of us, hear one day from a source established in another revered institution that the final solution had never occurred.

But to return to the witnesses. Only one, a Brooklyn woman, Rachel Berger, defied the decorous code of conduct to which the other witnesses had been so obedient. Time and again she responded with contempt, fairly spitting answers to the defense attorney's wealth of questions about time, calendar dates, distances in the camps. Then, unwilling to accept the mode of behavior in which the mention of retribution had no place, she informed the court and Mrs. Ryan's defense attorney in the course of her testimony that she would celebrate that day, the day she testified. She would celebrate it as a Jewish holiday, and dress up the way Braunsteiner and the other SS had dressed up when the SS doctors went through the ranks of Jewish prisoners and made their death selections. After the testimony of Rachel Berger, a witness so defiant of every courtroom propriety, the reporters crowded around and asked her the reason for her emotional behavior. Why was she there, a reporter asked. If the experience was so upsetting to her, what had made her come to court? The reply came in the faintly disbelieving voice one had heard so often from Holocaust survivors when they were confronted with questions whose import they could not fathom, whose assumptions were even more of a mystery. "Why, why I am here today?" She explained, then, what she had felt upon seeing the former SS vice-commandant in the courtroom, a sight which she thus described: "Gray suit immaculate, hair immaculate. Over her knees she had these two hands and her hands were so big, her legs so strong, so young. My whole family came to my mind. I remembered the eyes of my aunt, selected for the gas chamber, standing in line—a young woman, looking at me with such force, such eyes, as if to say maybe I could do something. My two classmates taken out during roll call because they had dysentery. I had a little cousin eight years younger than I. I remember once she came to my barracks at Majdanek and I found her kneeling down on the ground, all yellow, destroyed. And my little sister whom I loved, gassed. And here I see her, Braunsteiner, blooming! Sitting in this courtroom with those paws on her lap, folded. So strong, so fresh, so well looking."

Of such stuff are the memories of the Holocaust, the memories which shape, color and determine the lives of the survivors in so infinite a variety of ways. It is a truth known at one level or another to every Holocaust survivor that he inhabits two worlds, the world of the past and the world of the present, and that the logic of the first, the world of Holocaust memory, regularly makes that of the second, the present, absurd. It was perfectly relevant and proper to ask details of time and calendar dates in a courtroom, the survivor knew. Still, how absurd such questions, how absurd any effort to answer them when the queries referred to events at Majdanek or Auschwitz. A survivor tells of the experience of marching, near death from fatigue and starvation, in a long line of women prisoners headed toward Bergen Belsen. "I stopped," she said, "and there was a young SS guard next to me. Somehow, I forgot myself and I asked him, 'What day is this?' And for some reason he forgot himself and he told me, 'It's Wednesday.' I had nothing to lose and I asked him, 'What year is it?' And he forgot himself again and told me, 'It's 1944.' "

In the late 1940's and early 1950's, the time when most of the survivors arrived in the United States, they received their first proof that they and their experiences of the Final Solution were utterly incomprehensible to all who had not been a part of it. They learned that they might be asked by American friends and relatives what it was like to starve, and after being told that starvation was very bad, the friends and relatives might respond, yes they knew about that themselves because there had also been shortages of many things in America during the war, such as sugar. They had learned that relatives or others who spent the years 1939-1945 far from Europe's shores might ask a survivor to please search his mind, to relent, tell the truth and not exaggerate: surely sometime he must have been given a dessert after the main meal in the concentration camp. "Never even a piece of cake?" In the same period, the 1950's an Auschwitz survivor attended an alumni dance at her husband's law school, the husband being an American Jew whom she had met after the war. She noticed a man staring curiously at her from time to time and finally the man came over and introduced himself, confessing that he had seen the numbers on her arm. "I was wondering," the man informed her, "why you are wearing your laundry numbers on your arm." But what were they really, the man insisted. The survivor told him finally that the blue tattoo on her arm was a telephone number, whereupon the man departed, grateful, presumably, for having obtained an answer to his question. He was the dean of the law school, the survivor learned from her husband later in the evening. These encounters took place in the late 40's and early 50's, the time, it might be argued, when the consciousness of the world with regard to the facts of the Holocaust was still spare, unformed and thin. The trial of Adolph Eichmann, the event which provided the world with so complete and detailed a documentation of the Final Solution was ten years away, to come in 1960. In a work set in the late 40's, called "The Beginners," the novelist Dan Jacobson set forth the confrontation between Yitzak, a Holocaust survivor, and his Israeli cousin, Joel. Joel asked what Yitzak was doing with himself now and what he wanted to do. "To learn a trade, to get a wife, to get a flat," answered Yitzak. "I want everything you want." Yitzak spoke with an air of challenge as if the other wished to deny him what he wanted. And though Joel had no impulse to deny his relative what he wanted, he still felt deep within him an anguished question: "If a trade, a flat, a wife were all that Yitzak wanted, why should he have had to go through such experiences before he could think of having them? Having gone through such experiences should he not be thinking of other things? But of what, of what?" It was foolish to expect the survivors of the Holocaust to come out of the abyss with revelations, understandings, wisdoms, with any hope other than that of finding space for themselves, accumulating possessions, doing a job of work, establishing some order and privacy in their lives.

But if only it were so. If only it were so, as the novelist says, that survivors were not expected to come out of the abyss with revelations, understandings, wisdom. If only it were so that the survivors had only such sparing expectations of themselves as finding space, accumulating possessions, establishing some order and privacy in their lives. But, in truth, it was the fate of those who survived the Final Solution to bear the weight of special expectations, none heavier than those which they, the survivors, required of themselves. Having endured the unspeakable, suffered incalculable loss, incorporated images that would forever inhabit their mind's eye, it was nevertheless required of them, so they thought, that they be better, not worse, than other men—more generous, more idealistic, more understanding. A not altogether reasonable notion, this, that those who had suffered so at the hands of the world, who had been so abandoned by civilized society, should think in the end, this remnant of Jewry that had survived, that their duty was the betterment of mankind. It was not, then, simply finding space, accumulating possessions, establishing some order and privacy.

In truth, if it could not be said that the Holocaust experience had made the survivors more virtuous or more humane than other men, then it was undoubtedly true that some who survived had been hardened, their natures made dark by their experience. Still, the survivor was a man incapable of certain kinds of unconcern, incapable of the ordinary man's indifference to the tragedy of those far away. Whatever their political opinions, whatever sides they took, if any, in conflicts taking place far from these shores —Vietnam, Biafra, Bangladesh—the survivors of the Holocaust war were the same in this: they were always compelled to know the news of atrocity, to know it and believe it. They could not turn away, they could not attain to the onlookers' mentality. It was not a choice of good or evil in the survivors that made them capable of indifference. It was not a choice at all, it was a condition. Whether they wished it or not they would see what they might have wished not to see, to feel what it was most comfortable not to feel. To do otherwise was a luxury not permitted, especially to them. For did they not have special obligations as they saw it? They often spoke of this precept of theirs: What had they survived for if not to extract meaning from their experience, to be a light to the world? After all they had seen and suffered, some of them said, they had expected that there would come from the survivors a better sort of person, less selfish than ordinary, more sensitive to humankind. In this expectation, of course, they had been much disappointed for it was clear that the Holocaust survivors as a group had produced their fair share of people who behaved no better than anybody else and, in some cases, worse. Disappointments notwithstanding, in no group of people on earth was the sense of moral obligation to be found more deeply entrenched than in this one. They could be hard on one another in this regard, exceedingly harsh. Was not this one, this fellow survivor, too busy running around making money to remember where he came from? Did not this one busy himself getting rich, had not this one become a materialist, did that one ever give money to Israel, had they forgotten? They asked these questions again and again for they required proofs of themselves and of one another that though they lived normal lives now, normality had not made them disloyal to the past, material comforts had not made them oblivious, time had not made them, like everybody else, indifferent.

You will say, "How can one speak of all survivors as though they are one? Are they not different men, individuals with various attitudes, with different capacities?" True, the survivors of the Holocaust, those Jews who outlasted the efforts of the Final Solution, were individuals like any others. Still, there were not many among them of whom it could be said that they had no share in the central concerns of survivors, no share in certain passions, certain beliefs that were common to all survivors. They had endured, all of them, more or less the same fate, gone through more or less the same process of reentry into the normal world; they were Jews more or less. And what were these central concerns? Obligation, the sense of obligation however met. Another was the survivor's awareness, as he reentered normal life, that this normal life would not be his possession alone, nor even that of his newly acquired family. Rather, the new life would bear the weight of other hopes, other lives besides his own. The child he brought forth in the normal world, the child born in the DP camp or in Brooklyn, was not simply his child, but a symbol that the

Jewish people lived. The new normal life of the survivors would then bear the weight of other hope and other lives. There was the matter of the dead, millions who had perished. It was the survivor's obligation to tell, to testify, to live for those who had not survived, to tell and to testify even when weary, in order that the dead not be robbed of their voice.

Did ever a people attempt ordinary life while laboring under so extraordinary a set of requirements? The survivors had themselves, of course, lived only in order to bear witness; they had attested this many times. This wish alone, to bear witness, had made them endure when all other desire to live had gone from them. "The thing that I found so strange," one survivor has testified, "was that there we were in Auschwitz, fighting for life each day, and the greatest fear we had, the fear of the people around me, was not just of death but that every last one of us would die and there would be no one left alive to tell what had happened to us. It seems ridiculous now that when we needed every ounce of concentration to get a ration of bread, to get shoes, that we would be worrying about this."

What besides obligation were the other concerns of those who had lived? Normality, for one thing, that yearned-for condition which the survivors undertook to find after 1945. This quest was neither easy nor normal, for the Holocaust had given the survivors a schooling in the ways of the world, and the lessons they took from it were odd, unpredictable, and very often extreme. One survivor, Rebecca Spanner, made up her mind as soon as she and her husband arrived in America in 1949 that there were certain answers Americans expected to receive when they asked questions about what had happened during the war, and that those answers, and those alone, were the ones that she would give. A few nights after they had arrived in Texas, Rebecca went for dinner to the home of the American Jewish couple which had sponsored her. During the traditional and sumptuous Sabbath meal of fish, roast and chicken, her American hostess asked Rebecca how long it had been since she had meat. "Ten years," Rebecca told the woman promptly in obedience to her conviction that Americans wanted to hear such an answer rather than a truthful one which would have spoiled their notions of American bounty. "Ten years," the hostess marveled. She seemed highly satisfied, so it appeared to Rebecca. Later, much later, when she knew the woman better, Rebecca explained to her that after the war, with so many displaced persons in Germany, great quantities of food had been shipped there and there was plenty of meat, but at the beginning, new to the country and to her sponsor, she had been unwilling to intrude with these and other facts on what she considered to be the cherished beliefs of Americans. When she lied thus, it was without a pang of guilt, for she had learned that the proper attitude determined not only survival but the way that one got along in the world afterwards.

Survivors, however individualistic, were much the same in this, that they believed in the lessons they had taken from their Holocaust experience. The Holocaust tested and taught them, taught them to know the nature of men as they believed and to know it in ways not given to other people to know. The Holocaust was essential illumination and the authority for that which they knew in life. How could they not choose afterwards to utilize in their postwar lives that knowledge, that instinct, whatever it was, that they thought had helped them survive. Despite the fact that random chance had played so large a part in determining who would live and who would die (as survivors said themselves), there were other reasons for survival. Some survivors believed that they had lived because they had risked paths that other prisoners had been afraid to take; some because it had been their impulse to take a step backwards when everybody went forward; some because they had operated on the principle that when the Germans called for volunteers they would always step forward no matter what job the Germans might want them to do or where they would send them to do it. They made this choice on the grounds that any change in their condition was better than none. Others had had the impulse to keep to the rear no matter what, never to volunteer, to be the last if possible of any group being led by the Germans anywhere to do anything. The point of this instinct was reflected in one survivor's memory. "I don't know why. I always tried to go back, back, back. I knew nothing good could be waiting for me. Why should I be in a hurry to go first?"

What were some of these lessons, then, that the survivors took from their experience? One had learned that if you asked the person to kill you he would never do it, that asking for death robbed people of the will to kill you, though otherwise they would have killed you with no trouble at all. Another had learned that if you asked an enemy for mercy, it was better that the enemy should be a man rather than a woman because there was no chance at all with a woman. The women they had known as their SS captors, had invariably been crueler than the men. What else was the concern of the survivors? To find friends, links with the past, now that they had lost their families. "I was newborn," the survivors always said when describing the conditions they found themselves in after the liberation. This meant that they were, of course, happy to be alive, that they were ready to take up the life they had been given. But the phrase had a darker meaning, too, as they used it: "I was newborn." It suggested that those who had been left alive after the Holocaust were not only without place in the world and without possessions, but also had had no past life. For the roots and the ties of that life, the mothers, the fathers, the husbands, wives, children, holdings had been erased entirely. "It was as though I had not come from anywhere." And so the one link with the past was friends they had known in Europe. The friends took the place of relatives, the parents, husbands, brothers from whom the survivors had been separated, in trauma. Afterwards, twenty-five years after the final separation from loved ones, survivors wrestled with unanswered questions, unresolved quarrels, relationships, words spoken, not spoken, questions. Questions: How could one ask questions of the dead? Here is the memory of a survivor. "We were in Grössrosen and I was sixteen years old. I was put in a group with my mother and sixty other women. My mother was sick. One of the SS women came by our group and told us that we were going to be shipped to Auschwitz and the gas chamber on the next transport, and that we would not even stop at the main transfer for a selection. I was the only one in the group who was young and in good health. I said nothing to my mother. I stood with her. I went with her, but I resented it. I couldn't let her go alone, yet I did not want to die. What I wanted was for my mother to tell me, 'You stay and I'll go. You don't have to come with me.' But she didn't. Anyway, in the end, it turned out that we were only going to another camp." From another survivor: "I don't know why, but I think my mother always had the idea that I would come to a bad end or something, that I had some wild streak in me. I don't know why she thought that. In Auschwitz I held onto her as long as I could, and then she was gassed. Now when I think about her I wish there were some way to show her that I did lead an upright life, that I didn't turn out the way she thought."

Who were these survivors? The majority of them were between eighteen and thirty-nine at the time of their liberation by the Allies. Those who came to America arrived for the most part between the years of 1948 and 1951, a wave of immigrants unlike any that had ever come to these shores before. Included in this group were a large number of the professional classes, educated, those who would not have emigrated but for the catastrophe Nazism had wrought in Europe—artisans, lawyers, doctors, tailors, the highly educated, the barely literate. They have by now made their merger with the "normal" world insofar as possible. One says insofar as possible, for in the end, the survivor and the normal world must stay a distance apart. Consider, for example, the difference between the survivors' and the normal world's perception of the subject of Jewish resistance. Talk always turns to that issue. The most educated of them knew, and the least educated had heard about, the learned arguments put forth to explain how the Jews should have done this or that and thus and so when they faced the Germans. How they might have avoided losing so many millions had they been better, wiser, more foresighted. The survivors, the drygoods store clerk as well as the man of letters, knew the names of the historians on whose authority the world had come to believe that the Jews had been accomplices in their own murder. Having survived, they learned that there had grown up around the death of their families and their civilization a body of social theory to explain how it was that the catastrophe was in large measure the fault of the victims. The victims had not known how to behave in extreme circumstances, Bruno Bettelheim explained in "The Informed Heart." Raul Hilberg explained at length how the Jews had acquiesced in the design to destroy them and how Jewish psychology had contributed to this design. Hannah Arendt contended that the Jewish councils in occupied Europe, as well as organized Jewry the world over, particularly the Zionists, had actively aided the Nazi design for political reasons of their own. Hannah Arendt's was another and highly complicated form of the notion that the victims were accomplices in their own fate, that it was their own organization, not the Nazi will to implement the Final Solution, which had doomed millions of Jews. Bettelheim had asked, "Could not the millions of Jews have marched as free men rather than grovel? Why had the dead not died fighting if they had to die anyway? Why did they not grab guns?" Absurd questions, these, absurd in the face of the facts that had confronted the Jews of Europe. And still the survivors were not entirely able to treat them as such. The truth as they knew it themselves was that they had behaved in the way the armed might of the Nazis had dictated that an unarmed, helpless people behave. They knew that there had been bitter resistance and uprisings and that most of those who had risen up had in the end been killed, as had the unarmed and the helpless. Still, even with this knowledge, it was not possible for the survivors to ignore the widely heard opinion, that the Jews had gone "as sheep to the slaughter." Therefore, the subject of resistance churned frequently in the minds of the survivors. And whether they conceded wearily, as they often did, that armed resistance had mostly not been possible, or whether they marshaled evidence of armed resistance that did occur, the underlying fury of their response was the same and will so remain.

Much else remains as well for the survivors. It is now thirty-two years after the liberation. The sense of passing time haunts the survivors who still have the record to put straight, their testimony to give. With the passing of time, the impulse to record becomes more urgent, not less, the weight of memory heavier, the images in the mind's eye sharper. Some days ago I received in the mail an extraordinary document, fragments from the diary of a concentration camp. It was written by Dr. Paul Heller of the Abraham Lincoln School of Medicine in Chicago. Dr. Heller explained in the introduction why he should be occupying himself now with these notes and memories. "The first motive is the realization that the memory of this experience could not be extinguished, no matter how great my satisfaction with the normalcy of my private, professional and social life and the apparently successful creation of a new existence as a physician, an adaptation to a better world." This better world of which Dr. Heller writes has seen lately, among other things, the movies of Lena Wertmuller, in which the concentration camps of Europe—those camps through which millions passed to their doom—are treated as vehicles for black comedy. In this same culture, Marcel Ophuls is celebrated for a film, "Memories of Justice," whose chief distinction is its contention that the Allied governments who sat in judgment on the Nazis in Nuremberg were not better than the Germans they judged. The film offers, as well, easy equation of the American intervention in Vietnam with the crimes of the Germans under national socialism. This debasement of history, these ludicrous parallels, are themselves no small testimony to the strong revisionist impulse which exists in our culture today—an impulse, out of whatever political bias, to deny what was; out of whatever "artistic" yearning, to reinterpret, and in so doing, to lie. To so treat the history of 1939-1945, the history of the Final Solution, must, of course, be a particular temptation. It is a history that cannot be assimilated, though we have assimilated so much else. It cannot yet be absorbed that in this century there should have been an effort, largely successful, to exterminate a people. That the execution of this effort should have involved years of planning, hundreds of thousands of functionaries, of pieces of paper, of orders; that this people should have been scheduled in country after country to be separated, isolated from the rest of the population, deported, marched to trains from which they would be taken, men, women and children, prodded into lines for the gas chamber and their death. That this schedule should have been met efficiently enough is history of such a kind that we have been unable to put it away. So it is, and so it will continue; it is in the interests of our future that this is so. When this century's history has been written, however, what will remain are not the works of Lena Wertmuller, the alterations of the revisionists, or the up-to-date cliches of the political left. What will remain will be the imperishable eloquence of numbers tattooed on an arm.

Robert McAfee Brown

Theologian Robert McAfee Brown is professor of ecumenics and world Christianity at Union Theological Seminary in New York. He has written extensively on issues facing religion today and serves on the editorial boards of Christianity and Crisis, Theology Today and the Journal of Ecumenical Studies.

An authority on interdenominational matters, Professor Brown has served as an observer at the Second Vatican Council and is active in the affairs of the World Council of Churches. His book *The Ecumenical Revolution,* published in 1967, was given the first Sacred Heart Triennial Award for ecumenical literature.

A native of Carthage, Illinois, Professor Brown attended Amherst College, Union Theological Seminary and Columbia University. He has taught at Stanford University, Macalester College and Amherst.

Other books he has written include *Frontiers for the Church Today, Religion and Violence, Vietnam: Crisis of Conscience,* and *The Spirit of Protestantism.*

THE HOLOCAUST
AS A PROBLEM IN MORAL CHOICE
by Robert McAfee Brown

I approach this occasion with a mixture of eagerness and healthy dread. Eagerness because the occasion is an important one and I am deeply honored to have been asked to share in it; dread because the assignment outstrips my ability to deal with it, or indeed the ability of any theologian, however well-versed or eminent, to unravel the mystery of this most monstrous of all events in the annals of human evil; but healthy dread, as well, since an audience that has successively been exposed to Elie Wiesel, Lucy Dawidowicz and Dorothy Rabinowitz will already have gained enough insight to be generous toward the failings of anyone cast in the difficult position of following them.

How can one dare to speak?

How does one approach even the outer precincts of "The Holocaust as a Problem in Moral Choice"? How, particularly, does a Christian find an explanation when he remembers that Christians were among the chief participants, almost invariably on the wrong side? I have tried to expose myself to some of the literature and some of the persons for whom the Holocaust has been the normative event of our time, and have tried to enter into that experience in ways that on any human level I would have preferred to avoid. Yet, of course, both as a non-Jew and as a non-inhabitant of the camps, I cannot really "enter into" that experience at all. I can therefore hardly claim the right to speak about it. To some it may even seem a blasphemy that I dare to try.

This is a dilemma that has faced even those most personally involved in the Holocaust: how can one speak about the unspeakable? After having written half a dozen novels on the Holocaust, Elie Wiesel wrote a book called *The Oath,* in which he examined the notion that it might have been better to remain silent in the face of such evil than attempt to speak at all. The issue was a genuine one for him; if, after writing half a dozen novels, nothing seemed to have changed in human perceptions about the Holocaust, perhaps silence might have been the more powerful witness. *The*

Oath chronicles his realization that if, by the telling of the story of count-less deaths, one life can be saved, the story must be told, no matter how painful. If a single life can be saved, one must speak, even if in so doing one breaks (as did the narrator in *The Oath)* a sacred oath made half a century before.

That conclusion indicates why we must dare to speak of events our words will seem to trivialize if not distort. We must do so not only so that the dead are not forgotten; not only as a reminder that we, too, might have been able to play the role of SS guards and feel no inner laceration of the spirit; we must also do so as a way of seeking to ensure that such events can never happen again. For we must face the painful reality that there is that in our nature that could allow it to happen again, that could even will its repetition. And if retelling the story can alert us to such possibilities, and increase our resolve that they must be avoided, the retelling, however painful, must take place.

A variety of responses

I have discovered that there are many kinds of responses to the Holo-caust among both Jews and Christians. For Richard Rubenstein, the reality of Auschwitz has destroyed the reality of God. For him, no other con-clusion is possible. God, if God existed after Auschwitz, could only be a moral monster. For Emil Fackenheim, on the other hand, to engage in such a denial of God in the face of Auschwitz would be, as he says in *God's Presence in History,* to grant Hitler a posthumous victory: setting out in his lifetime to destroy the Jews, Hitler would finally have succeeded beyond his lifetime in destroying Judaism. For Elie Wiesel, to whom I shall shortly turn, the greatest problem posed by the Holocaust seems to be the silence of God. One may not have expected much from man; one surely could have expected more from God. Why did God not speak or act? Why did God seemingly remain indifferent? How can one do other than con-tend with a God so apparently callous?

There are also varieties of Christian responses to the Holocaust. These have been longer in coming and are only now beginning to receive sig-nificant articulation. Some Christians are not even willing to confront the issue; it is absent from their deliberation in ways that are harder and harder to understand. Others are so devastated by their discovery of Christian complicity in the event that they are immobilized by guilt. Still others react defensively, seeking to exonerate themselves and their Christ-ian heritage from any responsibility, usually by blaming it on others or letting a few brave Christians go bail for the massive numbers of indifferent and complicit. A few go so far as to assert that there has been an in-built anti-Semitism in historical Christianity that must be purged and replaced by a radical theological reconstruction.

Two overall problems

In all these responses, and others that could be noted if space permitted, there are at least two widely-shared problems. The first of these is the problem of *responsibility*. Who is to be held accountable? How widely must the net of accountability be spread? It includes Hitler. It includes Eichmann. Does it include the guards in the camps, the "good Germans" who only "followed orders"? Does it include those who knew what was going on and chose to remain silent? Does it include those who feared what was going on and took special pains not to find out? Does it include the Allied high command who, when told what was going on in Auschwitz, still would not give the order to bomb the railroad tracks leading to the death camp? Does it include the churches and the leaders of the churches who were silent even when many facts were known? This question of responsibility is a particularly burning one for non-Jews, though Wiesel and others have demonstrated that in this period there were even some Jews who preferred not to get involved—a fact I cite as a tribute to Jewish honesty rather than as a means of assuaging Christian consciences.

The second problem is one that all of us share—Jews and Christians alike—even though we approach it in different ways. This is the crisis of *belief* that the Holocaust forces on us. For who, whether Jew or Christian, can believe in a God in whose world such things take place? The perennial mystery of evil, the source of our greatest vulnerability as believers, reaches unique expression in the Holocaust. No theodicy can encompass this event so that its wounds are closed or its scars healed. It forever precludes easy faith in God or in humanity. Both are placed under judgment, and a verdict of acquittal may not be lightly rendered, if at all, to either party. (To this theme of the crisis of belief I will return toward the end of the present essay.)

The discipline of listening

How, then, are we to approach the Holocaust as "a problem of moral choice"? My first task as a Christian must be to listen, and to ask, "Who has the authority to command my ear?" Not the one who says it did not happen. Not the one who says it happened long ago, and we now have more pressing problems. Not the one who says it was only a temporary deviation from an otherwise reliable human norm. Not the one who simply theorizes. No, the one to whom I must first listen is the one who was there, the survivor, the one who knows it happened because he bears forever the scars, both physical and psychic, of the ordeal. In my case, listening to one particular survivor has been particularly important. He has been perhaps the most important single theological influence on me in the last four or five years, even though he makes no claim to be a theologian and prefers to call himself a teller of tales. He is Elie Wiesel. He has been wrestling with the moral dilemma of the Holocaust for a third of a century— he was deported to Auschwitz in 1944. He writes as a Jew and he insists that the more he speaks out of his own particularity, out of his Jewishness, the more he speaks universally to non-Jews as well. I can testify to that. He speaks to me.

His words are written out of fire and blood, the fire of the crematoria and the blood of the victims. So they destroy. Just as fire and blood are symbols of destruction, words nurtured by them produce destruction. They destroy illusions, complacency, indifference. But in both the Jewish and Christian traditions, fire and blood have creative possibilities as well. For fire can purge and blood can cleanse; they are symbols of new beginnings as well. So also with Wiesel's words. When their surgery has been accomplished—even while it is being accomplished— they become instruments of healing, reaching out over deep chasms of pain, not to anesthetize or to hide but to transform. Elie Wiesel's pilgrimage through his own "valley of the shadow of death" and beyond, through his series of wrestlings with the question of what we do in the face of the greatest moral obscenity of history—constitutes for me both a searing and a healing experience. As one who has first been called upon to listen, I propose to share some reflections on that listening, as I have had to walk, imaginatively, the path that for Wiesel was not imagination but ugly reality.

Wiesel's responses to monstrous moral evil

How does one respond, then, in the face of monstrous moral evil? We can distinguish at least five stages in Wiesel's pilgrimage.

The first response is the response not of a choice inwardly made but of a decision outwardly imposed. In the face of monstrous evil it may be that we are simply cast in the role of *victims.* This role is described in Wiesel's first book, *Night,* the autobiographical account of a boy of fifteen, loaded with friends and family onto cattle cars, experiencing the tortures of thirst and hunger and madness, the splitting up of families at the entrance to the camps, and the subsequent dehumanization to which all the "survivors" were subjected. Wiesel had been a pious Hasidic Jew, and on the very first night his Hasidic faith was destroyed. After being parted from his mother and sister forever, he walked into the camp with his father and discovered a large ditch from which giant flames were leaping. Wiesel writes, "They were burning something. A lorry drew up and delivered its load—little children. Babies!" (*Night,* p. 42). He knows that this is a nightmare, that it is not to be believed, that the terrible dream will come to an end. And it is indeed a nightmare, but it is in fact true, and Elie Wiesel will never wake up to find that its truth has been negated. And so, on that night, his childhood faith was destroyed: "Never shall I forget those flames which consumed my faith forever." (*Night,* p. 44) When morning came, he writes, "A dark flame had entered into my soul and devoured it." And the evening and the morning were the first day. Only the first day.

The rest of the journal italicizes the powerless and helpless role of a victim, the unwilling recipient of actions over which he has no control, in this case given unbearable poignancy because they are being etched in the life of a fifteen-year-old boy.

When the war ends, and he is finally released, Wiesel spends the first weeks of his liberation in the hospital at the point of death because, as he writes with crushing honesty, when the prisoners were released, all they could think about was food—and so got stomach poisoning.

> One day I was able to get up, after gathering all my strength. I wanted to see myself in the mirror hanging on the opposite wall. I had not seen myself since the ghetto. From the depths of the mirror, a corpse gazed back at me. (*Night,* p. 127)

One may unwillingly be cast in the role of victim. If there are any choices, it would seem preferable to be the *executioner* rather than the victim, and that role is explored in Wiesel's second book, a powerful short novel, *Dawn.* The narrator, Elisha, has "survived" the concentration camps at the end of the war, and while living in Paris is urged by Gad, a leader of Palestinian guerrilla forces, to go to Palestine to work for the establishment of the state of Israel.

Gad pleads all night long with Elisha. No longer, he argues, can Jews simply be the passive victims of historical fate. They must seize their fate in their own hands. He argues convincingly that the only thing to do is to go to Palestine with the guerrilla forces and engage in whatever terrorist activities are necessary to drive out the British and ensure the establishment of a Jewish state. And as dawn is rising in Paris, described as "a pale, prematurely weary light, the color of stagnant water," Gad looks out and says, "Here is the dawn. In our land it is very different. Here the dawn is gray; in Palestine it is red like fire." (*Dawn,* p. 31)   Elisha accepts.

They go to Palestine. Elisha is trained, participates in a raid and then, still very young, is chosen to shoot a hostage, John Dawson, who has been seized in reprisal for the seizure of one of the Palestinian leaders. The execution is to take place at dawn. Here is a reversal of roles; as Elisha goes down into the cell under the ground to do the deed, he can almost feel the Nazi swastika on his arm, as though he were now part of the SS troops he had abhorred. He would like to be able to hate John Dawson, because that might give moral meaning to the act, but he cannot whip up a frenzy. When the time comes that he must calculatingly pull the trigger, the shot goes through John Dawson's skull and Elisha comments, "That's it. It's done. I've killed. I've killed . . ." And then he says not "I've killed John Dawson," but rather, "I've killed Elisha." (*Dawn,* p. 126.) Although the victim has become an executioner, the execution turns out to be a self-execution. Murder is a form of suicide.

When Elisha goes upstairs to the Palestinian dawn, the dawn is not the dawn that Gad has promised, a dawn "red like fire." Instead, "The night left behind it a grayish light the color of stagnant water." It is still the dawn of Paris, not the dawn of the new country and the new hope.

So if it will not solve anything to accept the role of victim, neither will it solve anything to switch roles and become an executioner.

In a third book, which in the original French was called *Le Jour* (Day) but in English is called *The Accident,* we have another young survivor of the Holocaust, this time named Eliezer, Wiesel's own name, who is still trapped in a past he cannot escape. The "accident" is his being run over by a taxi, although he sees in retrospect that it was an accident only in the most euphemistic sense, since he realizes that he had willed not to step out of the taxi's way, and had welcomed the possibility of death as a possible escape from the past. He has seen himself only as a "messenger from the dead," among the living. He feels that he brings only death to those whom he confronts. He cannot find a way to escape from the past and affirm the present. He cannot bring himself to engage in a genuine act of love or sharing or commitment.

He has an artist friend, Guyula, who desperately tries to persuade him that this must be done—that he must choose the living rather than the dead, and ruthlessly, if necessary, stamp out the past. As Eliezer is recuperating in the hospital after the accident, Guyula paints his portrait. When the portrait is shown to Eliezer, it is clear that Guyula has ferreted out Eliezer's secret, his will to die. He pleads with Eliezer to love Kathleen and to let her love him; and then, to dramatize the need for a real break with the past, he lights a match to the portrait and burns it.

But it doesn't quite work. For when Guyula goes out, he leaves the ashes. The past is still there. The past is only destructive. There seems no way to stamp it out and begin again, free of its destructive grip.

Each of these first three books, then, leads into a cul-de-sac. It is only in the fourth book, *The Town Beyond the Wall,* that a new set of possibilities emerges. In this work, perhaps the most fruitful of all of Wiesel's writings, there are three further probings of the question. One of the options, madness, is creatively ambiguous; another, the option of spectator, must be utterly rejected; while the third, the option of participant, provides the beginnings of an extraordinary breakthrough.

On the flyleaf of *The Town Beyond the Wall* is a statement by one of Dostoevski's characters, "I have a plan—to go mad." And *madness* is explored as another way to deal with monstrous moral evil. Mad people are found in all of Wiesel's novels, often as the purveyors of the only true wisdom to be found within the works themselves. On close examination there seem to be two kinds of madness under discussion. (For this distinction, and many other insights within the present essay, I am indebted to a number of articles by Byron L. Sherwin.) There is what could be called "clinical madness," which describes those who simply give up, throw in the towel, and insulate themselves from the rest of the world, refusing to relate at all, living finally in total isolation. That, of course, is another cul-de-sac, a way without promise or hope.

But there is another kind of madness portrayed by Wiesel, what some have called "moral madness." This is the madness of those who said, in effect, "If this world of the Holocaust is to be described as a world of sanity, give me madness any day." When Wiesel himself went to the Eichmann trial in Jerusalem after the war, he was staggered with the ease with which it was possible to certify to the court that Eichmann was "sane." Wiesel wrote, in his *One Generation After:*

> It occurred to me that if he were sane, I should choose madness. It was he or I. For me, there could be no common ground with him. We could not inhabit the same universe or be governed by the same laws. (p. 6)

By the same logic, who in the world of the 1930's and the 1940's was sane and who was mad? Were those who were burning babies the ones who were sane, or were those who, for whatever reason, refused to sanction or be part of such actions, the ones who were truly sane?

Mosche, the "madman," was so described because he told people that Jews were being cremated, when everybody knew that such things don't happen in the twentieth century. Wiesel suggests, in other words, that the attitude which the world calls madness may in fact be the true sanity, seeing things as they really are, refusing to accept the values and patterns and standards that were regnant in Europe at that time. Such persons may have had a higher degree of sanity than those around them who called them mad.

So the response of madness, while ambiguous, is an ongoing response that needs increasing attention as a possible moral stance in the face of monstrous evil. For we too, in our era, have burned babies in the name of the American way of life—the napalm of the U.S. Air Force in southeast Asia is simply a more sophisticated weapon than the gasoline of the funeral pyres of Auschwitz.

Another role, one which Michael, the protagonist of *The Town Beyond the Wall,* rejects unambiguously, is the role of *spectator.* After the war, Michael returns to his home town of Szerencsevaros not quite sure why he does so but knowing that he must make his peace with the past in that place from which he had been deported by the Nazis a few years earlier. (Here is a significant advance beyond *The Accident.* Instead of trying to destroy the past, as Guyula had urged, Michael must find what salvation he can by confronting the past and meeting it head on.) Not until he revisits the town square, the scene of the earlier deportation, does the reason for his need to return become clear. Suddenly it clicks. He remembers that there was a face in one of the windows, an impassive face that watched the deportation with no sense of engagement, no sense of involvement. The face of a spectator. And Michael reflects:

> This, this was the thing I had wanted to understand ever since the war. Nothing else. How a human being can remain indifferent. The executioners I understood; also the victims, though with more difficulty. For the others, all the others, those who were neither for nor against, those who sprawled in passive patience, those who told themselves, "The storm will blow over and everything will be normal again," those who thought themselves above the battle, those who were permanently and merely spectators—all those were closed to me, incomprehensible. (p. 159)

The spectator still lives in Szerencsevaros. Michael talks to him and can discover no sense of passion or concern even after the event. And he makes an awesome discovery about himself. He discovers that he cannot hate the spectator, for, as he says, "Hatred implies humanity." All he can feel is contempt, a contempt which implies not humanity but something less than humanity, something decadent. It is noteworthy that the spectator realizes this and seeks desperately to be hated, because hatred will at least be an acknowledgment of his humanity and personhood. But Michael refuses to give him even that satisfaction.

For Wiesel, remaining a spectator is the most morally reprehensible response of all. The one who simply opts out, the one who will take no part, the one who will be neither for nor against, is not only inhuman, but is in reality *against,* for the spectator by his lack of involvement casts his vote for those who are doing the dirty work.

Where beyond these roles can one go? Wiesel develops a creative alternative in the latter part of *The Town Beyond the Wall.* It is a role that cannot be described by a single word like "victim," "executioner," "madman" or "spectator." But it is a role that can at least be pointed to by such words as "reciprocity," "identification," "sharing," perhaps even "love." Let us call it the role of *participant,* of one who decides, even in the face of terrible risk, to make an act of identification with another, to side with the victim.

This role is powerfully illustrated in two relationships in *The Town Beyond the Wall.* The first is the relationship between Michael and Pedro, a man with whom Michael begins to be able to relate as they build up a sense of mutual trust for one another—a quality that Michael, as a survivor of the death camps, had never since been able to feel toward another person. Pedro and Michael begin to discover that they can share, and that in sharing, their own identities become bound up with one another. As they are parting, Pedro says to Michael of their previous conversation, "I won't forget last night. From now on you can say, 'I am Pedro,' and I, 'I am Michael.'" (*The Town Beyond the Wall,* p. 131) Pedro can henceforth be identified only in relation to Michael, and Michael only in relation to Pedro. It is this sense of reciprocity, of participation, that frees Michael to be able to look at and engage in the human venture once again. He is soon called upon to test its reality.

Michael carries this precious truth with him into the prison cell in which he shortly finds himself incarcerated with a prisoner who has gone mad, totally cut off from the world, incapable of initiating any response whatsoever. Michael realizes that relationship must be established, or in a short time both of them will be mad. In an imaginary conversation, Pedro says to him, "Re-create the universe. Restore that boy's sanity. Cure him. He'll save you." (*The Town Beyond the Wall,* p. 182) This is the creative possibility that Pedro has offered to Michael in a compressed juxtaposition of five words: "Cure him. He'll save you." The mad prisoner needs

Michael. Michael needs the mad prisoner. They must find one another, enter into relationship with one another. And so Michael sets out to break through the recesses of madness to discover a point at which relationship can begin. For, as he says, "One of us will win and if it isn't me we're both lost!" (*The Town Beyond the Wall,* p. 185.) By various devices Michael begins to elicit little flickers of response from the other, enough so that he can say to the one who is as yet uncomprehending:

> One day the ice will break . . . You'll tell me your name and you'll ask me 'Who are you?' and I'll answer, 'I'm Pedro.' And that will be a proof that man survives, that he passes himself along. Later, in another prison, someone will ask your name and you'll say, 'I'm Michael.' And then you will know the taste of the most genuine of victories. *(The Town Beyond the Wall, pp. 188-189)*

And as the book ends, Wiesel writes of the prison counterpart to Michael, "The other bore the biblical name of Eliezer, which means *God has granted my prayer.*" (*The Town Beyond the Wall,* p. 189) It is highly significant that Wiesel gives to "the other" his own name—a clear affirmation that for Wiesel himself it is in relationship with another, in participation in the lot of the victim or potential victim, that a meaning can begin to be found that draws one out of the shell of isolation and depersonalized existence represented by the roles of victim, executioner and spectator.

At the end of this book night is receding and dawn is breaking, not the false dawn that greeted Elisha after he shot John Dawson, but the true dawn, full of fresh promise for a new day.

A way to summarize the extraordinary progression that has taken place in these books is to compare their endings. At the conclusion of *Night,* Wiesel looks into a mirror and sees himself as a corpse. At the end of *Dawn* Elisha looks out a window and likewise sees only a reflection of himself. He knows what this means, for he has been told by an old man ("mad," naturally) that if he looked in a window and saw a face, he could know that it was night—not dawn, not day, but night. At the end of *The Accident* Eliezer is looking only at a portrait of himself.

In all of those situations, the protagonist is still locked into himself, *seeing only himself.* But at the end of *The Town Beyond the Wall* he is looking into *the face of another,* and in that reciprocity, in that sharing, it is clear that creativity and healing have truly begun. Let us further note, as a transition to what follows, that at the end of the next book, *The Gates of the Forest,* the protagonist is in Williamsburg as part of a group that has formed a minyan for a service. He has found his way back to the midst of the Hasidic community. As the book ends, Gavriel is saying kaddish for his dead friend, giving expression to a relationship that extends beyond himself, beyond even another human being, to the God to whom the prayer is being offered.

Is there still a role for God?

I have tried to suggest that within the arena of the re-creation of human relationship and trust, Wiesel sees the possibility of rebuilding a life that has been destroyed by the Holocaust, and that in such sharing the reality of God begins once again to intrude.

But we must not jump to easy formulas or answers. It still remains difficult to talk about the Holocaust, difficult to talk about God, and even more difficult to talk about these together, without seeming to blaspheme. How can this ever be done?

Let us recall that for Wiesel it is the questions that count, not the answers. He is rightly suspicious of those who offer answers. He recalls a question to one of the participants in the Eichmann trial, in which the participant was asked if he could now discern a meaning in Auschwitz. The reply came, "I hope I never do. To understand Auschwitz would be even worse than not to understand it." Such a response is important. If we have a view of God into which Auschwitz somehow "fits," if we can conceive of a universe congruent with Auschwitz, then such a God must be a moral monster and such a universe a nightmare beyond imagination.

Nevertheless, for Wiesel and for many others the issue will not go away. He must *contest* with God, concerning the moral outrage that somehow seems to be within the divine plan. How can one affirm a God whose "divine plan" could include such barbarity? For Wiesel, the true "contemporary" is not the modern skeptic, but the ancient Job, the one who dared to ask questions of God, even though Wiesel feels that Job gave in a little too quickly at the end.

There is another way to approach the relation of God to the Holocaust. We must note that when Wiesel is writing about the relationship between person and person, he is also writing about the relationship between persons and God. Each relationship sheds light upon the other. The Hasidic tale with which he concludes *The Town Beyond the Wall* shows how this double dimension suffuses his writing:

> Legend tells us that one day man spoke to God in this wise:
> "Let us change about. You be man, and I will be God. For only one second."

God smiled gently and asked him, "Aren't you afraid?"

"No. Are you?"

"Yes, I am," God said.

Nevertheless he granted man's desire. He became a man, and the man took his place and immediately availed himself of his omnipotence: he refused to revert to his previous state. So neither God nor man was ever again what he seemed to be.

Years passed, centuries, perhaps eternities. And suddenly the drama quickened. The past for one, and the present for the other, were too heavy to be borne.

As the liberation of the one was bound to the liberation of the other, they renewed the ancient dialogue whose echoes come to us in the night, charged with hatred, with remorse, and most of all, with infinite yearning. (*The Town Beyond the Wall,* p. 190)

What happens (in Buber's phrase) "between man and man," also happens between man and God. And the qualities of the one relationship are likewise true of the other. In both relationships there is hatred. In both relationships there is remorse. In both relationships, also, there is infinite yearning.

Menachem, the believing Jew who was for awhile in Michael's prison cell in Szerencsevaros, is surely echoing Wiesel's own yearning question when he asks, "Why does God insist that we come to him by the hardest road?" (*The Town Beyond the Wall,* p. 146) Wiesel (who lived through Auschwitz) once had an exchange with Richard Rubenstein (who did not, but for whom Auschwitz meant the death of God and the consequent difficulty of living in a world where belief in God is no longer possible). Wiesel said:

I will tell you, Dick, that you don't understand those in the camps when you say that it is more difficult to live today in a world without God. NO! If you want difficulties, choose to live *with* God . . . The real tragedy, the real drama, is the drama of the believer. (Littell and Locke, eds., *The German Church Struggle and the Holocaust,* p. 274)

So if it is true that when Wiesel is writing about man he is writing about God, and when he is writing about God he is writing about man, we may retrace the human pilgrimage we took a few moments ago, and make the fascinating discovery that the roles Wiesel attributes to human beings in responding to monstrous evil are similar to the roles human beings have frequently attributed to God.

It is clear, for example, that many today believe with Rubenstein that in the face of the reality of the Holocaust, God has become a *victim.* A survey of the Holocaust and post-Holocaust world leads them to proclaim that "God is dead." The phrase, to be sure, was initiated long before the Holocaust, but the Holocaust has put the final seal upon the verdict; a God worthy of the name has not survived. God is victim.

There are others who, whether they intended it or not, come perilously close to describing God as *executioner,* God as the one who is finally the author of evil. This is a difficult conclusion for orthodox Christian theology to avoid, at least to the degree that logic inhabits orthodox formulations, for any theology that postulates belief in an omnipotent God has a difficult time evading the conclusion that an all-powerful God is ultimately responsible for evil. Such a God seems either to have willed, or decreed, or at the very least, "permitted" it.

There are some who would say that God is *mad,* a diabolical creator, or at least (in the other notion of madness we examined) a God who, like some of those who are humanly denominated as mad, has a totally different set of priorities and criteria for action. Wiesel, indeed, has written a play called *Zalman, or The Madness of God,* in which he sets forth the notion of a response to a God who makes demands so different from those of the world that those who respond will find themselves in grave difficulty with the world. Perhaps God and the world are simply incommensurate. That could be a consolation. It could also be a new source of despair.

The notion of God as *spectator* has frequently characterized human thinking about God; whatever else we affirm about God, we find that God seems to be aloof and removed from where we are. Either God can do nothing about evil in the world, or refuses to do anything about it. In either case, God becomes a spectator to evil. This, I think, is what Wiesel is wrestling with when he talks about the silence of God in the face of cries for meaning. And just as the human role of spectator seems the most morally culpable, so also would the divine role of spectator seem to be the most damaging charge we could lay against God—that the God who knew what was going on did nothing.

There remains the possibility of describing God as *participant* in the struggle with evil. This seems to me a possibility toward which Wiesel's thought has been moving. In the account of the reciprocity between Michael and Pedro, and between Michael and the silent prisoner, in *The Town Beyond the Wall,* we sense that in that give and take, that sharing, that risk-in-love, whatever has been meant by the word "God" is broodingly and hauntingly present. The theme is further pursued by Wiesel, not only in *The Gates of The Forest* and *A Beggar in Jerusalem,* but also in a yet later writing, *Ani Maamin,* which employs an even more direct use of Messianic imagery as a way of stating a demand that God share, at least, in the plight of creation. While we cannot pursue the themes of this remarkable poem in detail, we must note certain things that Wiesel emphasizes.

Ani Maamin is the libretto for a cantata Wiesel wrote that was set to music by Darius Milhaud shortly before his death. The words come from Maimonides' statement of faith, "Ani maamin beviat ha-mashiah"—"I believe in the coming of the Messiah." How, Wiesel asks, can a Jew still sing that song? Was it not lost in the camps? How is it that those who have hoped for a Messiah, who have hoped for a divine vindication in history, can continue to believe, when such belief has received no vindication? Could one *still* hope for a vindication? What does it take to bring the Messiah, if God really cares?

With such questions in mind, Wiesel retells the old Midrashic tale of Abraham, Isaac and Jacob going down from heaven to earth to find out what was going on, and reporting back to the divine throne. In Wiesel's version of the story, the terrestrial visitation occurs during the time of the Holocaust. The patriarchs report back to God. But no matter how loudly they talk, no matter how painfully they describe the horror, there is nothing but silence from the divine throne. Nothing but silence.

So the Messianic question for Wiesel becomes the question: *The world is so evil, why does the Messiah not come?* What does it take to bring him? Are not six million dead enough? And even if he came after six million deaths, would that not already be too late? That is the Jewish form of the question. But let us note that there is a Christian form of the question which is just the reverse. If the Jewish form of the question is, "The world is so evil, why does the Messiah not come?" the Christian form of the question is surely: *The Messiah has come, why is the world so evil?* In a presumably redeemed world, redemption is not so evident. Perhaps a time is coming when, at this point of their greatest division, namely their conflicting interpretations of the Messianic claim, Jews and Christians can begin to acknowledge that they are, among all the religions of the world, at least dealing with the same problem. Both acknowledge that a spectator God would indeed be a moral obscenity; that, somehow, to talk of love must mean to talk about participation and sharing.

And the extraordinary thing that happens at the end of Wiesel's drama is this: when the patriarchs have exhausted their patience and elect to return to the children of earth with a report of divine indifference, each tells the story of a Jew who continued to believe—who continued to believe *in spite of* everything, against all odds, with no conceivable reason to do so. And *this,* so the narrator informs us, breaks through the divine impassivity. The cumulative impact of the three stories reduces God to tears, tears of love. And as Abraham, Isaac and Jacob turn to go to earth, we are told:

> They leave heaven and do not, cannot, see that they are no longer alone: God accompanies them, weeping, smiling, whispering: *Nitzhuni banai,* my children have defeated me, they deserve my gratitude. *(Ani Maamin,* p. 105)

This is no *deus ex machina* victory that ties everything together. Wiesel immediately writes, "The Word of God continues to be heard. *So does the silence of his dead children." (Ani Maamin,* p. 105, italics added) But it is a powerful evocation of the theme of participant as a role we can be audacious enough to ascribe to God as well.

How, finally, do we "respond"?

We have looked at some of Wiesel's responses to monstrous evil: some may have no choice but to be victims; others, seeing evil's immensity, may capitulate and become evil's enablers, opting for the role of executioners; some may choose suicide or madness as attempts to cope with the problem; others may elect the ultimate cop-out of being spectators, or even the worse cop-out of pretending that the evil didn't really happen. Finally, some may insist that however feeble the effort may seem, it is crucial to side with those who are victims or potential victims and to do so in actions of participation, identification, and sharing, believing that only thus can there be created a counterforce whose very power, whose very unexpected power, may lie in its seeming fragility. Those who do so may or may not acknowledge that whatever terms they use, they will be wrestling with God, posing questions and remaining unsatisfied with answers, particularly answers that seem to satisfy and relieve them of further responsibility.

Woven into all those responses is a further response, mentioned early in these pages and so patent that we may almost have overlooked it. For we can also respond to monstrous evil by *chronicling it,* reporting it, reminding all listeners that whatever else they forget they may not forget *that* evil, lest they make its repetition possible.

Can one, however, chronicle a unique event—an event incommensurate with all other events—in such a way that it speaks to those in other situations? Some would argue that the very uniqueness of the Holocaust renders inappropriate any attempt to relate it to other events, lest it seem to be scaled down to just another instance of moral perversity.

I disagree. I want to test the reason for my disagreement, so that if I am wrong I can be further instructed. Start with the patent truth that we can never "justify" the Holocaust or, indeed, any instance of evil. We must always remain outraged, and resist the drift toward complacency that time and distance so easily induce. But continue with a recognition that we not only have an opportunity, but an obligation, to make use of the Holocaust for some kind of creative end. We point to good and positive events of the past as events that cast light on the rest of experience: Moses before Pharaoh saying, "Let my people go!" The Exodus and the giving of the Law, the prophet of the Exile singing "Comfort, comfort my people, says your God." Perhaps we need to point also to evil and dark events of the past. If we passionately exhort people to emulate great events, perhaps we must also passionately exhort people to repudiate dark events, to put them so far off that they can never be repeated.

It may be that the fires of Auschwitz are powerful enough to illumine otherwise dark corners of our moral landscape, making us aware of present acts of human demonry we would not otherwise see. Those fires have served a sensitizing purpose for Jews in relation to subsequent Jewish persecution in Russia, in relation to threats against the survival of Israel, in relation to anti-Semitic remarks that have recently emanated from the Pentagon. I think they can serve that purpose for the rest of us as well.

I have recently returned from a visit to Chile, Argentina and other Latin American countries. On the surface all seems well—just as on the surface all seemed well in Germany in 1933. But in the light of the fires of Auschwitz it was clear to me that all was *not* well in Chile and Argentina —just as all was not well in Germany in 1933. Arrests, "disappearances," confiscation, torture, all the marks of diabolical cunning, are present just below the surface, but not below the surface to those who can see. I think we are finally challenged by the Holocaust to the daring and frightening notion that an obscenity can be used as a way of forestalling other obscenities. If we can so affirm, then there is hope that the Holocaust, unredeemably evil in itself, could be a grotesque beacon, in the light of which we could gird ourselves against its repetition toward any people, in any time, in any place. *And I believe that unless we can use it as such a beacon, the Nazis have finally won.*

Wiesel and other Jews look to Israel as they make this point, but they look elsewhere as well—to Vietnam, to Chile, to the Sohel, to Bangladesh, to any place where people are suffering. I do not believe there exists a people who wants to say, "Only our pain is important." I believe there exists a people who not only wants to say, but does say, "Because of the magnitude of the pain we have suffered, we know that there is no pain anywhere that can be ignored. We know that pain everywhere must be combatted."

There is great wisdom in some advice offered by Azriel in *The Oath:* "So you hope to defeat evil? Fine. Begin by helping your fellow man. Triumph over death? Excellent. Begin by saving your brother." (*The Oath,* p. 14) For, as the narrator later says to us all, "Every truth that shuts you in, that does not lead to others, is inhuman." (*The Oath,* p. 73)

Can one, then, out of ashes and bitterness, affirm more than ashes and bitterness? Wiesel himself is proof that one can. He has earned the right to be heard. In the passage with which I conclude (from Littell and Locke, op. cit., pp. 276-77), Wiesel speaks to Jews, but as always, in such a way as to include the rest of us as well:

> When Rabbi Ishmael, one of the ten martyrs of the faith in Roman times, was led to his death, a heavenly voice was heard, saying, "Ishmael, Ishmael, should you shed one tear I shall return the universe to its primary chaos." And the Midrash says that Rabbi Ishmael was a gentleman and did not cry. And I couldn't understand that for quite awhile. Why didn't he cry? The hell with it! If this is the price to pay, who needs it? Who wants this kind of world? Who wants to live in it? Yet there are many reasons why he didn't cry.
>
> One, he was a martyr. Two, he obeyed. Three, the last and most poetic ultimate reason why he didn't cry was because he wanted to teach us a lesson in Judaism . . . Even while dying, he wanted to teach us a lesson: Yes, I could destroy the world and the world deserves to be destroyed. But to be a Jew is to have all the reasons in the world to destroy and *not to destroy!* To be a Jew is to have all the reasons in the world to hate the Germans and *not to hate them!* To be a Jew is to have all the reasons in the world to mistrust the church and *not to hate it!* To be a Jew is to have all the reasons in the world not to have faith in language, in singing, in prayers, and in God, but *to go on telling the tale, to go on carrying on the dialogue,* and to have my own silent prayers and quarrels with God.

Amen.